Divine Dowager

Saradamani at age 52

Divine Dowager

Life and Teachings of
Saradamani the Holy Mother

Narasingha P. Sil

Selinsgrove: Susquehanna University Press
London: Associated University Presses

Associated University Presses
2010 Eastpark Boulevard
Cranbury, NJ 08512

Associated University Presses
Unit 304
The Chandlery
50 Westminster Bridge Road
London SE1 7QY, England

Associated University Presses
P.O. Box 338, Port Credit
Mississauga, Ontario
Canada L5G 4L8

The paper used in this publication meets the requirements of the American National Standard for Permanence of Paper for Printed Library Materials Z39.48-1984.

Library of Congress Cataloging-in-Publication Data

Sil, Narasingha Prosad, 1937–
　Divine Dowager : the life and teachings of Saradamani, the Holy Mother / Narasingha P. Sil.
　　p. cm.
　Includes bibliographical references and index.
　ISBN 1-57591-073-X (alk. paper)
1. Sarada Devi, 1853–1920. 2. Hindus—India—Biography. 3. Ramakrishna Mission—Biography. I. Title.
BL 1280.292.S27S54 2003
294.5'55'092—dc21

2003004610

For *Sati*

. . . I consider [Saradamani] to be one of the greatest—nay, THE GREAT-EST, if you permit me to say—achievement of Sri Ramakrishna in this world. . . . Divine, yet human, a real woman, but saintly, the MOTHER has an irresistible appeal to me. She was so modest that only few could fathom her greatness while she was alive.

—R. B. Rybacov, letter to
Swami Lokeshwarananda
(30 November 1986)

Contents

Preface

My interest in the life and *logia* of Sri Ramakrishna Paramahamsa's wife, Saradamani, was aroused when I chanced to read in my undergraduate years at Presidency College, Calcutta, Achintyakumar Sengupta's imaginative biography *Paramaprakriti Srisri Saradamani*–an excessively idealized, obsequious account written in syrupy prose. However, the frequent use of hyperbole in mellifluous Bengali by one of the celebrated writers of the Kallol Yuga (the decades of the thirties and forties of the past century, named after the much acclaimed literary magazine *Kallol,* to which Achintyakumar was a prominent and prolific contributor), the Augustan age of Bengali literature, made an abiding impression on my adolescent mind. Though the populist biographer had made a veritable goddess of this simple and charming woman, his depiction of her character and behavior as the quintessential mother struck me as not only familiar but entirely realistic. I still recall Sengupta's concluding lines:

> We don't care to know so many things. We only know our Ma. No, neither a mother by consent nor a stepmother, nor even a fake mother, but a true, live mother. Like Mother Earth—kindhearted, bearer of all miseries, and remover of all sins. Let her punish or protect us, as she likes. We'll still call her our Ma even if she metes out punishment. We are happy by simply calling her our Ma. We do not care to know whether she has left us to encounter calamity or enjoy cornucopia. We only know that we are safe in her lap. Where would she abandon us? The whole world is her bosom. There is no place outside it. How much hardship could she create for us? How could our Ma rob us of our only glory, which is our Ma? What else would one care to ask for if he has his Ma?[1]

What impressed me as the most startlingly simple secret of Sarada's life when subsequently I read her biographies by several scholars, monastic as well as lay, is her natural ability to make adjustments without sacrificing individuality and thus relate to the wider world to be with other fellow humans. Unlike her celebrated God-man spouse or even his great disciple Swami Vivekananda, who had been convinced of the invincibility of their ultramundane spiritual insights and striven to teach them to the world, Sarada, as the spiritual mother of the Ramakrishna Order *(sanghajanani),* remained close to the mundane tribulations of human life and never insisted on imposing any one particular view or perspective on her disciples and devotees. I was particularly fascinated by the human skill of interaction that this unschooled woman of an unquestionably patriarchal society and monastic order displayed to retain her personal freedom and dignity. Her gut-wrenching earthiness and sheer plain commonsense and a serene disposition place her personality at once at a human and superhuman level, considering the social and spiritual ethos in which she grew up and conducted herself all her life.

While researching the biographies of Ramakrishna and Vivekananda I came across the rich corpus on Saradamani and decided to write on this third (for me the most interesting) of the trinity of the Ramakrishna Order. Sarada possessed neither her husband's ecstatic charisma and his funny and fun-loving disposition nor his disciple's good looks and great rhetorical skill, though her simplicity, tolerance, and fortitude never obscured her individuality and convictions. This is a remarkable combination of character traits that are hard to find in the life and work of the two male members of this holy trinity. My determination to investigate Saradamani's life and my two articles on her elicited a comment from a fellow scholar (who must remain anonymous), noted for his imaginative creativeness, that my enterprise reveals some "oedipal strains" in that in my studies on Ramakrishna and Vivekananda I have "slain the Father and attacked the Brother (Vivekananda)," but in my Sarada project I seem to be "very much in love with the Mother!" I enjoyed the punch that was delivered "with a grin," though I happily debunk his estimation of Saradamani as the "frumpy village girl [who] became a Goddess."

All Bengali sources consulted for this study are cited in my own translation, unless otherwise stated. I am very grateful for the long conversations I had with the foremost monastic Sarada scholar, the erstwhile editor of *Udbodhana,* Swami Purnatmananda. I came to know from him (through my conversations with the swami on 24 August 2000) that there are no archival materials for Sarada; all the materials that can be procured are from the published accounts available at the bookshops of the Ramakrishna Order as well as other stores in Calcutta.

In this connection I would like to inform readers, with great regret, that the general secretary of Sri Ramakrishna Math, Belur, Howrah, denied my request for permission to cite from one of the publications of the Ramakrishna Order directly in my book. He apparently suspected a sinister "design" in the title of my book, especially my use of the word "dowager" for Saradamani, and told me point-blank concerning my earlier books on Ramakrishna and Vivekananda that "instead of feeling proud of these great souls, . . . [I was] desecrating our Motherland" and hence denied my request. I have, therefore, been forced to paraphrase my own translation of several, including the one in question, for the sake of honoring ther copyright, though sadly the Math's decision has deprived my work of the opportunity to showcase the insights of a distinguished Sarada scholar freely and fully. However, I have tried my very best to render the paraphrased lines not only meaningful and interesting but also true to the spirit of the original. Needless to mention, I have retained a number of direct quotes from the sources for which permission was obtained and from others following the "fair use" parameter defined by the Copyright Act of 1989 and by my publishers.

On a happier note, however, I express my heartfelt gratitude to Swami Prabhananda, secretary to the Ramakrishna Mission Institute of Culture, Calcutta and a renowned scholar in his own right, Swami Satyavratananda of Udbodhana Karyalaya, Calcutta, Swami Jnanananda of Sri Ramakrishna Math, Mylapore, and to Bandana Puri Devi, Nandita Puri Devi, and Jayanti Puri Devi of Sri Sri Saradeswari Ashram, Calcutta, for their generous permission to use the materials published by their respective institutions. Thanks are also due to the organizers of the conference "Encountering Kali: Cultural Understandings at the Extremes," Barnard College, Columbia University (20–22 September 1996), the Western Conference of the Association for Asian Studies, Boulder, Colorado (25 October 1997), and the Thirty-second Bengal Studies Conference, Indiana University, Bloomington (2 May 1998). I particularly enjoyed the wit, enthusiasm, and appreciation of my audience and the generous hospitality of the organizers of the last-mentioned forum.

Acknowledgments

I am grateful to the Faculty Development Committee of the Western Oregon University for two Major Project Grants that facilitated my travel to and research in Calcutta.

I thank the following individuals for their permission to use materials published by them:

Editors of *Asian Journal of Women's Studies* (Ewha Womans University Press, Seoul, Korea), *Numen* (E. J. Brill, Leiden), and *The Journal of Religious Studies* (Punjabi University, Patiala, India);
Director, Associated University Presses, Cranbury, New Jersey;
Director, the University Press of America, Lanham, Maryland;
Swami Satyavratananda of Udbodhana Karyalaya, Calcutta;
Swami Prabhananda of the Ramakrishna Mission Institute of Culture, Calcutta;
Swami Jnanananda of Sri Ramakrishna Math, Mylapore;
Bandana Puri Devi, Nandita Puri Devi, and Jayanti Puri Devi of Sri Saradeshwari Ashram, Calcutta.

It must be understood, however, that their permission constitutes in no way their concurrence with the interpretation of this author.

I also thank the anonymous readers of the Susquehanna University Press for their constructive critique of my draft and their suggestions for improvement.

I am profoundly indebted to Wyatt Benner for his excellent copy editing, which has enhanced the quality of the text and notes enormously, to say the least.

Finally, I extend my gratitude and love to my wife, Sati, who gracefully endured my weekend trysts with the Holy Mother and shared the household chores belonging exclusively to my domain. Appropriately, I thus dedicate this book to her.

Chronology

Birth	22 December 1853
Marriage and first visit to Kamarpukur	May 1859
Second visit to Kamarpukur	December 1860
Sarada's relief work during the famine at Jairambati	1864
Third visit to Kamarpukur	May 1866
Fourth visit to Kamarpukur (Ramakrishna and his mother Chandramani at Dakshineshwar)	December 1866–January 1867
Fifth visit to Kamarpukur (Ramakrishna's tantric *sadhana* with Yogeeshwari)	May-November 1867
First visit to Dakshineshwar	March 1872
Sodashi Puja	5 June 1872.
Return to Jairambati (illness)	Middle of 1873
Death of Ramchandra Mukhopadhyay	26 March 1874
Second visit to Dakshineshwar	April 1874
Back at Jairambati (dysentery)	September 1875
Attack of dysentery and invocation of the goddess Singhavahini	1875
Jagaddhatripuja	November 1875
Death of Chandramani	27 February 1876
Shambhu Mullick builds Sarada's home	11 April 1876
Return to Jairambati	November 1876
Third visit to Dakshineshwar (encounter with the *dakat baba* at Telo Bhelo)	17 March 1876
Return to Jairambati	November 1876
Jagaddhatri Puja at Jairambati	14 November 1877
Fourth visit to Dakshineshwar	February 1878
Return to Jairambati	Sometime in late 1878 or early 1879

Fifth visit to Dakshineshwar, accompanied by Lakshmimani and Shyamasundari	February 1881
Return to Jairambati with Shyamasundari	March 1881
Sixth visit to Dakshineshwar	February–March 1882
Seventh visit to Dakshineshwar	January 1884
Eighth visit to Dakshineshwar	March 1885
Ramakrishna's terminal illness	April 1885
Ramakrishna's mandate to Sarada	1886
Ramakrishna's death and Sarada's vision of her deceased husband	16 August 1886
Leaving Cossipore home and stay at Balaram Basu's place at Baghbazar	21 August 1886
Pilgrimage to Brindaban from Baghbazar	30 August 1886
Return to Calcutta	31 August 1887
Return to Kamarpukur and hardship there	September 1887
Visit to Balaram Basu's home	May–June 1888
Pilgrimage to Puri	5 November 1888
Return to Calcutta	12 January 1889
Visit to Antpur in the company a number of Ramakrishna devotees, including Narendranath	5 February 1889
Return to Kamarpukur	12 February 1889
Visit to Calcutta and stay at Belur	January 1890
Death of Balaram Basu	13 April 1890
Bloody dysentery and relocation to Baranagar	August–September 1890
Return to Kamarpukur and Jairambati	October–November 1890
Girish Ghosah's visit to Jairambati	April–May 1891
Vivekananda's departure for the United States	31 May 1893
Stay at Belur retreat of Nilambar Mukhopadhyay	June–July 1893
Return to Jairambati	(?) October 1893
Visit to Calcutta and departure for Kailowar with the family of Balaram Basu and a few devotees of Ramakrishna	January–February 1894
Return to Jairambati	April 1894
Second pilgrimage to Brindaban	February 1895
Return to Jairambati	13 May 1895
Visit to Calcutta (59/2 Ramkanta Basu Street)	April 1896
Transfer to a three-storied storehouse at Sarkarbadi Lane on the riverbank at Baghbazar	May 1896
Vivekananda's return from the West	19 February 1897
Advance payment to purchase land for building a *math* at Belur	3 February 1898

Ramakrishna Math relocated from Alambazar to the house of Nilambar Mukhopadhyay, Belur	13 February 1898
Registration of the land for Belur Math	5 March 1898
Sarada visited by Swamiji and his three Western female disciples	17 March 1898
Building construction at Belur starts under the supervision of Swami Vijnanananda	April 1898
Sarada participates at the opening of Nivedita Girls' School at Bosepara Lane	13 November 1898
Monks of Ramakrishna Order start living at Belur Math	2 January 1899
Vivekananda returns to the West	20 June 1899
Death of Sarada's brother Abhaycharan	2 August 1899
Visit to Jairambati	30 October 1899
Radharani, daughter of Abhay's widow born Sarada's illness at Kamarpukur	26 January 1900
Travel to Calcutta	October 1900
Return of Vivekananda from overseas	9 December 1900
Sarada participates in Durgapuja at Belur Math	18–22 October 1901
Death of Vivekananda	4 July 1902
Stay at Jairambati	November-December 1903
Stay at a rented home at 2/1 Baghbazar Street	14 February 1904
Pilgrimage to Puri	November–December 1904
Return to Calcutta	January 1905
Death of Sarada's mother Shyamasundari	January 1906
Death of Gopaler-ma	8 July 1906
Kedar Das donates land at Gopal Neogy Lane (presently 1 Udbodhana Lane) for building a permanent home for the Holy Mother	18 July 1906
Travel to Jairambati for Jagaddhatri Puja	October 1906
Return to Calcutta and participation in the Durgapuja at the home Girish Ghosh	October 1907
Building construction begins at Gopal Neogy Lane under Swami Saradananda's supervision	11 November 1907
Transfer of Udbodhana Office to Matrimandir (Mother's Temple)	Late 1908
Travel to Kamarpukur to celebrate Ramakrishna's birthday	1909
Travel to Calcutta with Saradananda	21 May 1909
Contracts smallpox	June 1909
Indisposition	6 October 1909

Travel to Jairambati	16 November 1909
Return to Calcutta	July 1910
Travel to Kothar, Orissa, estate of Balaram Basu. Initiates a Hindu Christian convert after restoring his Hindu identity	Early February 1911
Sojourn to southern India	Late February 1911
Return to Calcutta	11 April 1911
Last meeting with Nivedita	12 May 1911
Travel to Jairambati	17 May 1911
Radhu's wedding at Jairambati	10 June 1911
Death of Swami Ramakrishnananda	21 August 1911
Death of Sister Nivedita	13 October 1911
Presence at Durgapuja at Belur	16 October 1911
Pilgrimage to Baranasi	5 November 1911
Return to Calcutta	16 January 1913
Dysentery attack	June–July 1913
Construction of Jagadamba Ashrama at Koalpara	1914
Travel to Jairambati	19 April 1915
Home constructed at Jairambati	15 May 1916
Travel to Calcutta	8 July 1916
Travel to Jairambati	31 January 1917
High fever at Jairambati	8 January 1918
Arrival of Swami Saradananda, Drs. Satish Chakravarti, Jnanendranath Kanjilal, Yogen-ma, olap-ma and Saralabala Sarkar from Calcutta for Sarada's nursing	21 January 1918
Recovery and relapse	10 April 1918
Recovery	17 April 1918
Travel to Calcutta	5 May 1918
Death of Swami Premananda	30 July 1918
Travel to Jairambati	27 January 1919
Travel to Calcutta	24 February 1920
Illness and treatment by Dr. Kanjilal	28 February 1920
Treatment by Kabiraj Shyamadas Bachaspati	12 March 1920
Treatment by Dr. Bipinbihari Ghosh	8 April 1920
Death of Swami Adbhutananda	24 April 1920
Diagnosed with Kala Azar fever by Dr. Prandhan Basu	16 May 1920
Death of Sarada's brother Baradaprasanna	20 May 1920
Death of the Holy Mother	21 July 1920

A Note on Bengali Orthography and Calendar

I have decided to avoid diacritics with a view to rendering the text more reader-friendly. For purely Bengali words and phrases, I have used the soft *b* in place of the Sanskritized *v,* which is used for all *tatsama* (Sanskritized) Bengali terms. In case of proper nouns, I have followed conventional orthography for the more familiar names, words, and phrases, such as Vivekananda, deva, devi, and the like, and used Bengali orthography for all others. The publication date for most Bengali sources marked with B.E. stands for Bengali Era, which follows the Gregorian calendar by 593 years, 3 months, and 14 days in reckoning time. For example, A.D. 2003 coincides with 1410 B.E.

Divine Dowager

1

Introduction

Jananim Saradam Devim Ramakrishnam Jagadgurum
Padapadme tayoh shritwa pranamami muhurmuhuh.

[I prostrate and pray again and again at the lotus feet of Ramakrishna
the Teacher of the World and Sarada the Divine Mother.]

—Prayer of Sarada's disciple and biographer
Durgapuri Devi, in *Sarada-Ramakrishna*

I

SARADAMANI CHATTOPADHYAY (1853–1920) WAS AN OBSCURE, SEMILITERATE CHILD-
bride of Sri Ramakrishna Paramahamsa (Gadadhar Chattopadhyay, 1836–
86), the famous ecstatic priest of the Kali (Bhavatarini or "Deliverer of the
World") temple at Dakshineshwar (some five miles north of Calcutta). The
story of her travails and tribulations as the wife, and later widow, of a celebrated celibate ascetic husband and her eventual transformation into Holy
Mother, indeed a veritable goddess, rendered her the subject of innumerable studies by devotees and admirers, and even by some academicians,
who have unilaterally and universally applauded and even theologized her
pain and suffering as her highest contribution to Hindu femininity. Ironi-
cally, however, the story of Sarada's life remained practically unknown
during the lifetime of her famous *paramahamsa* spouse, who stole the lime-
light. Her existence and activities were mentioned only obliquely and casu-
ally by the Calcutta *babus* as part of the colorful accounts of Ramakrishna's
ecstatic behavior, which included frenzied devotional and ecstatic dancing,
singing, and getting into a state of samadhi. In his biography of the *thakur*
(that is, "Master," the popular way of addressing Ramakrishna), Max Müller
refrained from commenting on Sarada's conjugal life with the caveat that
no one had any right to complain against it, because "she was satisfied with

23

her life," even though his contemporary, the Brahmo leader Protap Chunder Mozoomdar, had blasted the celibate *paramahamsa*'s "barbarous treatment" of his young wife.[1]

After her death on 21 July 1920, Sarada's brief vita was published in *Prabuddha Bharata* (September 1920) and in *Vedantakeshari* (October and November 1920). Her first noteworthy biographical sketch was published in *Prabasi* by the noted journalist Ramananda Chattopadhyay (Baishakh, 1331 B.E.), who mentioned two distinct types of the late Holy Mother's biography: those by her devotees, based on their insights and the "dialogic process," and those by objective and nonpartisan scholars. In his biographical sketch Chattopadhyay, however, clearly mentioned the multiple qualities (such as wit, selflessness, and practical common sense) of this woman who could live up to the training reportedly imparted by her ascetic husband. But, though she was trained by her husband, she did, nevertheless, contribute immensely to the success of his ascetic life. Like Max Müller, Romain Rolland, in his biography of Ramakrishna, praised Sarada's adaptability, ingenuity, and selfless assistance to the spiritual exercises of her ascetic husband.[2]

In 1953, the year of Sarada's birth centenary, two accounts of her life were published in English–*Great Women of India,* edited by Swami Madhavananda and Dr. Rameshchandra Majumdar (Calcutta), and *Women Saints of East and West: Sri Sarada Devi (The Holy Mother) Birth Centenary Memorial,* edited by Swami Ghanananda and Sir John Stewart-Wallace (London). In the historian Majumdar's estimate, Sarada was respected by people not just as Ramakrishna's wife but rather as his true disciple. Majumdar went on to observe that she exemplified the quintessential qualities of Indian womanhood. In her article on Saradamani in *Women Saints of East and West,* Ms. Vijayalakshmi Pandit, the first woman president of the U.N. General Assembly, observed that Sarada, as the custodian of her family's faith, was a woman of all times. The most recent "scholarly" study of Saradamani has concluded on the basis of a sentence from the *Bhagavad Gita* that she "was cosmic energy, sakti or maya incarnate."[3]

Sarada's immaculate conjugal life has been shown to be an ideal example of sublimated sexuality in two analytical studies in *Prabuddha Bharata* (Ramakrishna Order's major journal in English), Holy Mother Birth Centenary Number. C. T. K. Chari's psychological analysis argues against the Freudian paradigm by claiming that both Sarada and her ascetic consort together demonstrated how sublimated sexuality helped elevate humanity to a higher spiritual plane. Dr. Muthulakshmi Reddy even posited that many problems facing modern India, such as family planning, birth control, and the related social and financial woes, could be solved in the light of the sacred conjugal life of the celebrated duo.[4] In his essay "Bharatiya

Samaje Nari-Dharma" [Duties of women in Indian society] in *Udbodhana*, the order's highly popular weekly publication in Bengali, Dr. Sudhirkumar Dasgupta considered the Holy Mother as a perfect example of the ideal woman, excelling in the eternal ideals of fidelity to and love for her husband, motherhood, and spiritual life. Most important, as Dasgupta maintains, Sarada's amalgamation of the ideals of motherhood and spirituality demonstrates her own genius and not her husband's training.[5]

II

Amidst the cacophony of loud paeans sung for the all-suffering Holy Mother, not a single voice of remorse can be heard for the trials and tribulations of this sweet-natured rustic woman, whose childhood had been devoted to performing sundry labor-intensive chores at her parental home and whose youth was sacrificed at the altar of her husband's patriarchal asceticism. A little over a decade ago, an editorial of the *Prabuddha Bharata* unhesitatingly declared that her "personality is a wonder of this age" and proclaimed her the model of modern womanhood in the most hyperbolic prose.[6] Her most popular modern biographer and a former editor of *Udbodhana*, Swami Purnatmananda, declared as late as 1997, echoing his predecessors, that Saradamani is Sita reborn for the sake of India's, even the world's, welfare.[7] In an earlier study the same author had postulated a theology of Sarada's human pain and suffering by declaring that she was an incarnation of the all-suffering but stainless *(shuchismita)* Sita, "the eternal ideal of Indian women," and was born to demonstrate this ideal in modern India.[8]

The entire corpus devoted to this woman's life succeeded in dehumanizing, deifying, and consequently denaturing the story of a simple but industrious and intelligent woman who had been a victim of her God-man husband's whimsy as his dutiful wife, an object of obsequious adoration by his disciples and devotees as a widow, and the subject of a colossal mythology constructed by hagiographers after her death. In tome after tome, both in Bengali and in English, routinely produced by the Ramakrishna Order, the human face of the historical Sarada is hidden behind the petrified effigy of a goddess, recipient of gratuitous panegyric as the Mother of the Universe *(jagajjanani*, a popular appellation for the goddess Kali) or as the Holy or Divine Mother *(Srima)* by the devotees of a patriarchal society.[9] Swami Saradananda's admonition to an eager devotee of Sarada who had expressed a desire to publish her biography is the most telling testimony to the careful construction of the Holy Mother's idealized image. "I've gone through your manuscript on the Twice-blessed Mother," the swami wrote to the young author and an intrepid devotee of Saradamani, Labanyakumar Chakravarti.

> In my estimation, this manuscript, if published, will purvey an antagonis-
> tic, even a very poor image, of the one on whom people like you and me
> shower all our devotion and yet remain unsatisfied. You're a skilled writer,
> but you must learn how to write on some topics that will be intelligible to
> readers and how to select publishable episodes. It is important to keep your
> pen under utmost control at times. Slowly you'll learn all the things and
> you'll excel in writing. It is necessary to ascribe some . . . incidents of
> [Holy Mother's] life to other people. Try to learn this and write thus–do not
> hasten to get your book published right away. I'm telling you all this only
> because you're a disciple of the Twice-blessed Mother and therefore one of
> us.[10]

It is thus not easy to penetrate the mist of apotheosis and mystification and gain access to the odyssey of a real human being.

III

This study seeks to achieve an almost impossible goal–to rescue the human Sarada from the Holy Mother or the Divine Mother of a century-old legend and examine the process of her deification. This author questions the traditional hagiographical claims for Saradamani's incarnational status like that of her famous *paramahamsa* spouse and instead posits that a close look into her conversations and the eyewitness accounts of several devo-tees may not only help us explain her divine motherhood but also acquire an understanding of Saradamani as an individual. However, I wish to make it clear that this study does not intend to debunk the raison d'être or legiti-macy of sacred biography. I do recognize the cultural and theological sig-nificance of Hindu hagiography, which since around the sixth century B.C.E. has been showcasing the lives of saints and the *mahatmans* (great souls) as "a divinely established paradigm, the recurrent return to earth of God in human form at a time of the decline of righteousness."[11] Hagiographies, as Reynolds and Capps maintain, are "an extraordinary form of biography because they recount the process through which a new religious ideal is established and, at the same time, participate in the process."[12] It is also instructive to recall the recent comment of a scholar of Hindu hagiography:

> While hagiographies are a treasure-trove of information about saints, the
> study of hagiography has often been frustrating for scholars seeking his-
> torical facts, for despite their mutual concern with the lives of saints
> hagiographers' aims are much different than those of the scholar construct-

ing a critical historical biography. Where some scholars seek facts that will constitute a factual account of the saint's life, the hagiographer has often blended these facts in an intricate mix of myth and legend.[13]

My own aim is to study Saradamani's humanity, and hence I examine her odyssey as a historical personality and I seek to show her sacrifice, suffering, striving, and success in a patriarchal society and a highly hierarchical and patriarchal monastic order. Dr. Khandelwal observes in her interesting study of a female saint, Anand Mata, that ascetic women glorify maternal values, and thus, for them, "motherhood [has] to do with intimacy, food, scolding and compassionate love."[14] I find Saradamani, though not an initiated *sannyasini* (nun), a true exemplar of this motherhood which she privileged over renunciant discipline, and one who earned her celebrity as a Holy Mother, even a veritable goddess. The success and significance of Sarada's holy motherhood has to be comprehended in the context of the culturally sanctioned status of Hindu women as well as the evolving concept of Hindu (especially Bengali) motherhood of her times. It will not do to see Sarada as a silent (meaning, somewhat dumb) rustic spouse of a God-man—one whose deification was the result of uncovering something concealed or concocted or of "perfecting . . . silence," as has been imagined in a quasi-fictitious portrayal of this no-nonsense, practical woman.[15] Though her elevation to the position of *sanghajanani* was facilitated by one of her husband's influential disciples, she had a legitimate claim to this exalted status, because she just merited it. An erstwhile judge of the Calcutta High Court has observed that the Holy Mother's leadership and personal example contributed to the collegiality and camaraderie displayed by the monks of the Ramakrishna Order.[16] A distinguished historian has remarked shrewdly that Sarada's personal qualities "cannot be understood by studying [merely] the historical context of her society and period, because . . . [they] mirrored her own individual magnanimity."[17]

IV

In the patrifocal Hindu culture upheld by the brahmanical tradition, women are confined to two major social roles: wife and mother. The ideal woman is a *sadhwi* who obtains her liberation from the cycle of samsara by dedicating *(sadhana)* her life to her husband and family. Indeed, in the Hindu texts "the highest respect and appreciation are reserved for the mother. . . . In motherhood, women achieve symbiosis with the earth and nature on the one hand and with the Great Goddess, the cosmic mother, on the other."[18] The idea of a divine mother who is the source of creation is found in the Vedas (1500–300 B.C.E.) and in a number of later religious texts known as the *puranas* and *agamas* (4th–5th centuries C.E.). Foremost among these texts was the *Markandeya Purana*. Thereafter the cult of the Great Goddess developed its theology and rituals in a number of exegeses.

During the first quarter of the first millennium of the Christian era, monotheism made its appearance in Hindu texts. The supreme deity, the creator and savior possessing cosmic energy, was Shiva or Vishnu–both male gods and both totally transcendent. The *Upanisads* (c. 800–300 B.C.E.) speculated on the existence of a transcendental truth or reality–the essence of all phenomena, as well as the irreducible center or self of all living beings. This transcendental reality, Brahman, is the supreme God *(ishwara)* who is the creator and sovereign controller of the cosmos and of living beings. In the tantric and *shakta* texts on the margins of orthodox Vedic tradition, Shakti is conceived as a cosmogonic and cosmological feminine principle with a view to relating the supreme God to the creation. She is the source and cause of creation, continuation, and cancellation of the material as well as of the spiritual cosmic order. As the *Kenopanisad* has it: "Kenesitam patati presitam manah. Kena pranah prathamah praiti yuktah" [*Prana* and *mana* are, respectively, the external material *prapancha,* or the phenomenal order, and the spiritual *prapancha,* or the spiritual order].[19] The Ishwara or Brahman is *purusa* (male), inactive, and passive consciousness. Shakti, on the other hand, is ever changing and ever active. Procreation is brought about by the union of the male and the female, and the creation of the phenomenal order is correspondingly caused by the communion of Ishwara and Shakti. The divine will is expressed through and acted out by her. Yet she is autonomous and rules creation through her multifaceted power. Thus she is the supreme Godhead who wields her divine power through myriads of secondary powers or goddesses.

However, though Shakti has power, it is derived from the authority of the supreme being. Shakti is God's spouse. In tantric theology, enshrined in the *Devi Mahatmya*, composed in the sixth century C.E., there developed the idea of the cosmic feminine principle as the sexual partner of God, giving birth to creation. This divine sexuality of the goddess is equated with divine power that is beneficial and nurturing–the Mother Goddess. But Shakti also has a deluding dimension, *maya,* and as *maya* she is the great divine aggressive force, bringing divine righteous rage against the transgressor of cosmic moral laws. *Maya* also seduces humankind into the bondage of transitoriness. Thus the Mother Goddess possesses a seductive personality as well as a motherly quality of compassion. Full of love for her children, she provides them with ways and means of receiving her grace. It can easily be seen that the paradigm of femaleness is reflected on all the different levels of the cosmic principle of *shakti.* Shakti is wife and mother— *matrika, jagajjanani.* She also combines the masculine-feminine principles—*Shiva-Shakti samarasa*—equating Shakti with creation as well as with the Absolute by virtue of her unity with Shiva.

The concept of the goddess reveals the understanding of feminine nature in a patriarchal society controlled by the brahmanical ideals. All three aspects of the goddess—*prakriti* (undifferentiated matter of Nature), in other words, Mother Nature; *shakti* (energizing principle); and *maya* (seductress)—are linked to her sexuality and allocate a dual social role to woman as wife and mother. From her childhood a girl is groomed for her role of wife and mother, and her sexuality is placed at all times under the culturally constructed and socially sanctioned control of the male. In a society where "caste membership is entirely dependent on patrilineality" motherhood "is highly extolled as the fulfillment of a woman's social life." Both the *dharmashastras* (rules of right conduct) and the magisterial *Laws of Manu* (c. 200) stress the dual character of the Hindu female, her *shakti* and *prakriti*, and prescribe methods of controlling female behavior.[20] Hence a wife who is a mother is considered to be the bestower of all good fortune to her husband and children, and she is deemed to be immensely auspicious *(sumangali)*." Her widowhood, however, is deemed inauspicious. As a widow, a woman has the potency but no proper channel of realizing it without her husband. Thus her potency needs to be controlled at all times. That is why she is forced to lead a harsh, regimented life like that of a convict accused of a heinous crime.[21]

In Hindu tantric tradition (c. 500–c. 1000) the world is conceived in terms of sexual polarities: *prakriti* (female) and *purusa* (male). The female pole represents *dynamis* and *energia,* whereas the male pole stands for pure consciousness *(theoria)* and is passive. The *purusa-prakriti* duality is represented by such personalized divinities as Shiva-Shakti, Vishnu-Sri, or Radha-Krishna. However, unlike the Samkhya system (historically related to, though older than, the tantra), which emphasizes the *purusa-prakriti* polarity, in the tantric worldview both poles are united. As Jacobsen explains, "according to Tantrism everything inheres ultimately in the consciousness principle which is both knowledge and activity, and therefore everything is consciousness. . . . Tantrism is therefore ultimately monistic. . . ."[22] In Tantrism, thus, male and female poles complement each other and merge into one. The social implication of this theological construct is that male and female are equal, because each has necessary functions that are not superior or inferior to those of the other. Man and woman possess equal dignity, because together they constitute the social world, just as in their theologized, abstract forms they together constitute ultimate reality.

However, though the tantra recognized the equality of male and female, this pristine ideal has not realized itself in real life.[23] Indeed, Swami Vivekananda was quite right in the remark he made in a letter to his friend

Haripada Mitra. As the swami reminded Mitra, a true *shakta* does not care for drugs and drinks but regards women as the manifestation of the supreme energy of the world, which is Ishwara. He added further that women are thus regarded in the West. It is Westerners who actually act up to Manu's admonition: "Yatra naryastu pujyante ramante tatra devatah" [God's grace manifests where women are respected]. Quite appropriately, Westerners are prosperous, educated, and enterprising. Sadly, the people of Manu's India harbor a contemptuous attitude toward women and are thus unenterprising, poor, and slavish.[24]

Gender discrimination in real life has its imprimatur from religion in that the Hindu goddesses have little to do with female equality with the male. "It is not to be expected at all that balanced 'egalitarian' dialectic between male and female follows the Indian goddess, if only because India does not share Western ideologies of *homo* [*et mulier?*] *aequalis*," Penelope McKibbin reminds us.[25] In fact, Hindus believe in a variety of male-female relations. Husband dominance is highlighted in the ascetic Shiva; wife dominance is privileged in Shakti subduing Shiva, as can be seen in the iconography of Kali; and male-female equality is shown in the iconography of Ardhanarishwara. The male is viewed as self-controlled, while the female is viewed as undisciplined and wild, needing control and management. Contrary to what Westerners would like to see, Indian women believe in order, because they hope to gain more powers in an orderly universe. An orderly woman is vastly superior to and stronger than an orderly man.[26]

Such attitudes are deeply ingrained in the culture of the Hindus. The women in the *Mahabharata*, though obliged to practice a stricter standard of morality than men and though they lived under male protection–under fathers until marriage, husbands after marriage, and brothers, if not married–yet enjoyed much freedom. They moved about freely and participated in public festivities and feasts. There are references in the epic to "fair ladies flocking to festive gatherings," Professor Apte informs us.[27] Asha Lata Pandey adduces the examples of Vedic women such as Ghosha, Apala, Lopamudra, Vishwvara, Surya, Indrani, Yami, and Romasha, who were highly educated and some of them renowned scholars. Pandey also writes: "In a theosophical debate between Shankaracharya and Mandana Misra, the latter's wife was appointed to be the judge–obviously because of her superior knowledge and spiritual attainments."[28] In fact, as Sister Hughes writes, in the epic literature of Vedic India and Celtic Ireland one notices

a society in which women enjoyed respect and protection, in which they were represented as enjoying certain freedom and fulfilling many different roles. Their anger was feared, their jealousy was destructive, their courage undaunted and their love and tenderness sought after and cherished.[29]

Women of the *Mahabharata* such as Gandhari, Kunti, or Draupadi were *virya-nari* (warrior women) par excellence. They would expect their spouses to be valorous and virtuous, and they would exhibit a great sense of dignity and self-respect when threatened with shame and dishonor. To cite the Sister once more: "[T]he Indian woman in her home, as cherisher of the family, as educator of her children and helpmate of her husband, is Lakshmi, but when these are threatened, she is Mahadevi too."[30] The noted French anthropologist Georges Dumézil writes of the trivalent Hindu goddesses who incorporate three functions: maintenance of cosmic moral order; protection and defense; and enhancement of prosperity, fecundity, and beauty of all living beings. Hughes finds King Yayati's daughter Madhavi in the *Mahabharata* to be a true exemplar of trivalent capacity.[31]

V

Bearing in mind the cultural construction of womanhood briefly reviewed above, let us try to situate Saradamani's life both as a widow from a traditional household and as a cultural icon of Hindu Bengal in the context of the historical moment during which she flourished as a public figure. The nineteenth century, especially its latter half, witnessed not only the consolidation of the British Raj but also the colonial response to the political, economic, and cultural domination, celebrated in Indian history (especially in Bengal, the headquarters of the Raj) as the Bengal Renaissance. One aspect of the so-called Bengal Renaissance as a movement of modernization that is germane to our study is the "women's question."[32]

Originating as early as the late eighteenth century, this movement had undergone a significant change by the third quarter of the nineteenth. The liberal, nationalist, and egalitarian reform movements of the early renaissance were triggered, albeit in selective ways, by Western contact and impact. The later period saw a shift from rationalist to nationalist enterprise, and the liberal modernizing tendencies gave way to a conservative parochial mood with a view to positing an indigenous paradigm of cultural autonomy and self-respect in opposition to the Enlightenment paradigm of modernity imposed by the metropolitan West upon the colonies.[33] In this process the *bhadralok* (the urban middle-class or upper-class) nationalists of Bengal produced a discourse of dichotomy between the inner and the outer, the inner designating an ideological and idealized moral-spiritual domain and the outer a highly schematized material domain. The moral-spiritual domain represented the social space of home and the material that of the world. The home was the sphere of the woman, and the world that of the masculine and powerful imperialists. The home was the domain of the colonized East par excellence, which the imperial West had failed to conquer. This domain was hermetically sealed against the Western influences and thus preserved the authentic identity of the colonized Indians. It is in the context of this dichotomization that the model of the modern Indian woman was constructed.

While recognizing the need for the reform and education of women—a fallout from Western influence—this model harked back to an indigenous ideal of womanhood that emphasized women's essentially spiritual (that is, feminine) virtues such as modesty, humility, gracefulness, compassion, devotion, and sacrifice. These pristine virtues were reincarnated in the colonial period as orderliness, thrift, cleanliness, and skill in managing domestic finance and administration as the virtues of a *bhadramahila* (feminine form of *bhadralok*) to be inculcated by modern education. However, the ideal woman of nationalist discourse—the new woman—was a highly disciplined and better-qualified stalwart of the hegemonic norms of a new patriarchy. This patriarchy exercised its dominance through subtle persuasion and invoked the image of woman as goddess and mother—an image that "served to erase her sexuality."[34] The Bengali mother was thus mythicized. As Jasodhara Bagchi has observed, "[T]he ideology of motherhood strengthened the social practice of hidden exploitation of women."[35]

VI

In the last quarter of the nineteenth century patriotic Bengali literature—both of the middle-class and of the Grub Street varieties—highlighted the figure of the woman in conceptualizing the motherland or *deshamata,* personified as the Mother Goddess, such as Kali and Durga. Here also, as Tanika Sarkar has demonstrated, the historical patriarchal agenda found its fruition through the mediating figure of a divine female or an abstracted female as the *deshamata.* The goddess was to arouse her sons, the *santans,* a select band of ascetic warriors who would engage in the final battle for liberation. If the duty of the Mother Goddess was to prepare her sons for the battlefield, the mother at home was to cultivate morality and discipline with a view to restoring and maintaining orderliness. The mother of the household was the new patriotic woman, whose duties ended when her sons grew up to join the host of the moral-patriotic army. She was not to be militant herself, but she had to be the mother of heroes. Following the ancient Hindu tradition, Indian nationalistic history of the nineteenth century thus constructed an idealized womanhood by and for the patriarchal society.[36] This nationalist ideal simply glorified the traditional role of woman as the begetter and nurturer of heroic sons.[37] Thus even though she was apotheosized and celebrated for her maternal power and even though, since the sixth century C.E., she was accorded a "supremely important role," as is evident in eloquent doxologies and hymnologies, womanhood was in practice diluted "into the more self-sacrificial and digestible holiness of motherhood."[38]

Yet women of colonial Bengal did exert themselves to be a true *sahadharmini* (co-upholders of *dharma*) in the contemporary sense of the term. A recent study of advice manuals for women in the nineteenth century highlights a proactive response on the part of Bengali women to the patriarchal dominance of their husbands, who in turn had to cope with the domination of colonial masters. As Girijaprasanna Raychaudhury's (1862-99) two treatises of this genre—*Ramanir Kartavya* [Women's duties] (1884) and *Grihalakshmi* [Domestic goddess] (1890)—reveal, women were exhorted to be educated and to rise above romantic and erotic fantasies. As Judith Walsh concludes,

> [I]t is clear from these two "Advice for Women" texts that changed conditions of study and employment led the Western educated to want adaptations in their home relationships. In *Griha Lakshmi* and *Ramanir Kartavya* we see two aspects of this effort at adaptation; in both books women's lives, their relationships and even the worlds they inhabited are being re-conceptualized; they are being re-imagined so that they complement the demands of study and employment that their husbands face in the outside world of British ruled India.[39]

Raychaudhury's paradigm of womanhood found its clearest articulation a generation later–in Panchanan Bhattacharya's prosopography published in 1921–extolling the positive feminine virtues of purity, benevolence, constancy, fidelity, self-abnegation, self-respect, duty, and honor, as well as the modern virtues of patriotism, religious devotion, saintliness, public spirit, and service to fellow humans.[40]

2

Saradamani's Early Life

She [Sarada] was quite artless. She was simplicity incarnate. She never
fell out with anyone during playtime.

—Aghormani Devi (Gopaler-ma)

I

BIOGRAPHICAL DETAILS OF SARADA'S EARLY LIFE PRESENT PROBLEMS PRIMARILY
because of a paucity of direct evidence or eyewitness reports. The extant
sources repeat the account emanating from Sarada herself. This is particularly problematic in that she herself provides a typical hagiographical interpretation of her miraculous birth, marriage, and adulthood. This she must
have internalized from the life story of her saintly spouse. Thus she claimed
that her birth mirrored that of her husband, Ramakrishna. According to her
story, her mother, upon her return from Sihore, where she had visited a
particular temple, squatted under a tree to relieve herself. Her stomach felt
full, as if a gust of wind had penetrated it. She kept squatting there and
soon beheld an extremely pretty little girl of five or six dressed up in red
silk cloth *(lal cheli para)* who alighted from the tree and wrapped her tender arms around the woman's back saying: "I have come to visit your home."
Her mother instantly fell senseless and had to be carried home. That little
girl entered her womb, and Sarada sprang from that fetus.[1]

She was born on 22 December 1853 into a poor brahmin family of
Jairambati village in the district of Bankura in what is now the state of West
Bengal. She was named by her mother Kshemankari [the Auspicious One],
but her aunt changed her name to Saradasundari (alias Saru). The lower
caste neighbors addressed her as Thakrundidi (Thakrun is feminine for
Thakur, Ramakrishna's appellation, and *didi* means elder sister). Her parents were deeply religious people, the father, Ramchandra Mukhopadhyay,
being a devotee of Rama (paralleling Ramakrishna's household deity

Raghuvira, another appellation for Rama). He was a small farmer and a priest of the community, which consisted mostly of nonbrahmin families such as milkmen, barbers, blacksmiths, and confectioners. Ram and his wife, Shyamasundari, were a simple-hearted, pious couple. Although Shyamasundari was quite generous to her neighbors and often fed them sumptuously, she and her spouse never accepted gifts from others. On the other hand, Ram often accosted passersby, inviting them to his home for a smoke. As Sarada recalled later, her mother was a hardworking housewife who always kept her home neat and clean. Shyamasundari used to say that her home belonged to God and His devotees.[2]

Typically, nineteenth-century Bengali village life was marked, as now, by religious rites, folklore, and legends. Sarada recalled that as a child she used to be accompanied by another girl just like her, who used to help her in all her chores, such as collecting weeds for cattle fodder from the river, carrying rice to the workers in the field, bathing her brothers in the river, and the like. However, this companion used to disappear on seeing people coming near Sarada.[3] This story was obviously meant to convey the message that young Sarada's mysterious companion was the goddess herself. The child Sarada grew up absorbing the piety of her community, playing with toy gods and goddesses, especially Kali and Lakshmi, and fantasizing about the various exploits of the divine beings of folklore. As one of her biographers has written, "[S]he was thus going through her lessons in the kindergarten of religion."[4]

II

According to the testimony of Sarada's more ordinary childhood companion Aghormani (a.k.a. Gopaler-ma), Sarada was "simplicity incarnate." Even while playacting the housewife in some feminine games, she never crossed any playmate's path or engaged in altercation. On the other hand, "when other girls fell out, she would mediate, settle their quarrels, and reestablish cordial relations."[5] Another acquaintance of Sarada's recalled that since her childhood Sarada was diligent in work, intelligent, quiet, and well-behaved. She never had to be told what to do. She was resourceful enough to perform her duties with meticulous care. Naturally kindhearted, the eleven-year-old Sarada worked tirelessly trying to cater to many hungry families during a terrible famine that ravaged her community in 1864. She often did cooking for her family even at a tender age when she lacked the strength to lift the pot of boiling rice from the clay stove *(unan)*.[6]

III

At the age of six, in May 1859, Sarada was given in marriage to Gadadhar Chattopadhyay, who hailed from the neighboring village of Kamarpukur. A priest of the Kali temple at Dakshineshwar, some five miles north of Calcutta, Gadadhar, (later to be known by his famous adopted name Ramakrishna), was a young man of twenty-three at the time of his marriage. This apparently incongruous match between an infant and a full-blooded youth has been mythologized. According to the myth, the little girl chose him for her groom when she sighted him at a musical soiree in Sihore, her mother's native village. Ramakrishna is also reported to have told his mother, who was searching for a suitable bride for her son, that he would only marry that child who had chosen him as her future husband. The point for this sort of mythologizing is that Sarada's marriage to Ramakrishna was preordained, that is, a match made in heaven. At the time of his marriage, Ramakrishna was known to have been a victim of some sort of mental derangement because of his reportedly severe ascetic exercises. Stories of his trances and ecstasies at Dakshineshwar had reached his home at Kamarpukur, and his employers as well as his widowed mother, Chandramani, feared that his mental condition, an outcome of severe continence, would be improved if he got married. Finding a suitable girl from a compatible caste family for a "mentally deranged" young man proved problematic, and hence Ramakrishna's mother decided on the only available match even at the cost of paying the girl's father a hefty bride price *(kanyar maryada)* of three hundred rupees.[7]

Ramakrishna, of course, duly earned the nickname of *ksyapa jamai* or "crazy son-in-law" by the people of Jairambati, his in-laws' village. Whenever he would visit Sarada's parental home, the village women would blow a conch shell *(shankh bajato)* and spread holy water on the path along which they would escort him to his wife's home. We are told that the reason for Ramakrishna's ceremonious reception by the residents of Jairambati was their attempt to cure Ramakrishna of his malady by their ritual.[8]

IV

Sarada never had any formal education. She did accompany the neighboring children to the village *pathshala* (elementary school) and thus learnt some of the alphabet. Later, at Kamarpukur, her in-laws' home, she learned to read the primer *(barnaparichay)*. Unfortunately, her self-motivated educational effort was nipped in the bud when her husband's nephew, Hridayram Mukhopadhyay, confiscated the book, declaring that women must not engage in learning. Sarada, however, procured another book and took lessons from her husband's niece Lakshmimani. As she said, she had a chance of concentrating on her education at Dakshineshwar much later, following her ailing husband's relocation to Calcutta (Shyampukur Street) for treatment.[9]

Like most girls, she harbored two feminine desires: to wear gold ornaments and to become a mother. These two commonplace feminine aspirations were to be fulfilled in her life in an unusual manner, resulting in her eventual deification as the Holy Mother adorned with the accoutrements of a married woman. We are told how as a six-year-old bride of the twenty-three-year-old Ramakrishna, Sarada refused to part with the bridal ornaments that her mother-in-law had borrowed to adorn her during the nuptial ceremony. Even after she had attained adulthood, Sarada continued to be fascinated by gold. Her husband, who had been preaching the merits of giving up *kamini-kanchana*, that is, "woman and gold (or wealth)," declared that she was a goddess and, as such, wished to be bedecked with jewelry; and he bought her gold armlets and bangles. It must at once be noted that Ramakrishna's decision concerning his wife's gold bangles was probably taken when his young wife had come to Dakshineshwar in great panic after she had heard the canard of his divine madness *(dibyonmad)*. Thus the present of the ornament was not only meant to keep a gold-loving female satisfied but also meant to make the simple and pious rustic woman believe that she indeed was a goddess and thus above human frailties and carnality.

Ramakrishna's shrewd strategy to keep himself out of harm's way, that is, out of the expected husbandly duties of a married man to his wife, was right on the mark. Sarada, indeed, was very fond of gold, and perhaps her husband's ascetic indifference led her to sublimate her erotic impulses by developing a love for ornaments. Even after her husband's death on 16 August 1886, the thirty-three-year-old Sarada failed to give up ornaments, contrary to the custom of Hindu widowhood. She had her way by reporting a vision and a dream in which she claimed to have been commanded by her late husband, who had died a religious celebrity, to continue to wear ornaments like a *sadhaba* (married woman), because his passing away was not his "death."[10] Shortly thereafter, during her pilgrimage to Brindaban, she had a vision of her husband in dream in which the latter commanded her not to take off her bangles, and declared that he was Lord Krishna himself and therefore she was forever a married woman.[11]

Convinced that her husband was not dead but was ever present, she always wore bangles and red-bordered *sari* in defiance of people's admonition that wearing ornaments was as unbecoming of an ascetic's wife as it was of a widow. Even some of her devotees and disciples spread a canard

that Sarada not only wore gold bangles, but even wore *sindur* (the vermil-
ion mark of a Hindu woman whose husband was alive)—an embarrassing
situation that prompted the president of the Ramakrishna Order, Swami
Madhavananda, to remark that one must take what some of the Holy Mother's
disciples say with a grain of salt, because they often spread baseless rumors.[12] To defend herself from further cultural criticisms, Sarada drew upon
her own folk culture. She performed the rite of *panchatapa* (penance with
"five fires") for seven days, which sanctioned her rather unusual behavior
for a Hindu widow.[13]

From the sparse information available on Saradamani's childhood and
adolescence, it may be safely surmised that she had a humdrum, unevent-
ful life in the sleepy little village of Bankura district. Her time was passed
mostly staying at home, helping her family in domestic chores, though she
also enjoyed the company of a handful of playmates, all girls, with whom
she had some innocent fun. At one time she might have had some contact
with the Vaishnava Kartabhaja sect of her village.[14] It was her remarkable
and fortuitous marriage to Ramakrishna that catapulted a rustic maid into
fame in the *bhadralok* society of metropolitan Calcutta. Until her ritual
worship by her husband in 1872, young Sarada's early life gave absolutely
no hint of her future celebrity, contrary to the pious accounts of her sacred
biographers.

Sri Ramakrishna Paramahamsa (1836–86)

3

Saradamani's Husband, the Married Celibate: Ramakrishna's Sexuality

> Have you no shame? You have kids and yet you don't mind copulating
> with your wife! It's sheer bestiality! Don't you hate mucus, blood, piss
> and shit, and the like? One who meditates on the lotus feet of God
> regards even the prettiest woman as mere ash of the cremation ground.
> How could anyone fancy a body that will not last and is made up of
> such dirty stuff as worms, filth, and phlegm! Aren't you ashamed of
> yourself?
>
> —Sri Ramakrishna to SriM

I

SARADA'S OTHER FEMININE DESIRE, AFTER SHE CAME OF AGE, WAS TO BECOME A
mother. But her strange marriage transformed her into the wife of a husband whose antipathy to sexuality deprived her of any possibility of achieving normal motherhood. There is indeed an ironical truth in Swami
Nirvedananda's observation that "Ramakrishna's behaviour towards his wife
. . . beats all records. It is strange, unprecedented and obviously beyond the
range of human understanding."[1] Admittedly, his marriage was partly the
outcome of parental pressure and his employers' insistence. Once he told
his visitors in a reminiscing mood: "Oh, what a state I was in! When I was
first overwhelmed by this condition [divine madness], I had no idea how
days and nights passed. Everybody said that I was crazy. That is why they
got me married."[2] It is noteworthy that while his elders thought of marriage
as an antidote to an illness caused by unnatural and excessive continence,
Gadadhar had his own reasons for getting married. Years later he told a
devotee jestingly, "Do you know why a man like myself needs a wife? You
see, who would have taken so much care to prepare foods suitable for my
stomach? Tell me, who would have provided so much comfort for my
body?"[3] Ramakrishna's devotee biographer, of course, provided a rather

41

lengthy theological and teleological hermeneutic of the Master's marriage, which, to be brief, he interprets as a divine *lila* intended to teach the world the real meaning of detachment and the real significance of *brahmacharya* in married life–the spiritual foundation of Hindu social life.[4]

In the eight years following her marriage in 1859, Sarada had been to her in-laws' home four times for a total stay of less than three months. Her husband had left his village in late December 1860 and did not come back home until May 1867. However, when she turned a teenager by 1867, she was alarmed at the rumors of her husband's return to Kamarpukur with a *bhairavi* (a female practitioner of tantra) named Yogeshwari and with his nephew Hridayram, who had by now become his factotum and looked after his ecstatic uncle.

The episode of Ramakrishna's spiritual practice with Yogeshwari is enveloped in mystery and mystification, especially in his biography by his perfervid devotee Ram Datta, which contains lurid details of his "very scary" and "extremely horrible" practices with the *bamni* (*brahmani*, that is Brahmin woman, as Ramakrishna used to call Yogeshwari). Over the years, various writers, including Jeffrey Kripal, have built an elaborate mystical and tantric explanation of this experience, the authenticity of which is difficult to determine.[5] What one can gather about the Master-*bhairavi* story is that Yogeshwari suddenly appeared at Dakshineshwar, apparently from nowhere, sometime in 1861. She probably was a professional *bhairavi* from the region of Dakshineshwar, which abounded in numerous *bhairavi chakras* (*bhairavi* circles). She appears to have a rather mysterious and muddy past, and we have Datta's admission: "We have heard many tales about the *brahmani* but we hesitate to divulge them to the public."[6] Ramakrishna was greatly impressed by the *bhairavi* and the various books she carried with her.

Most probably, the woman had some plan for herself and the young priest. She reportedly taught her eager but utterly confused disciple sixty-four tantras, including *sadhana* with "the skulls of five creatures, including that of a human being," which she procured personally.[7] Subsequently she tried to train him in *sodashi-puja*–the tantric ritual with a young female. Ramakrishna, of course, found the required act for this ritual—that of a *vira* or a hero (that is, ritual copulation with the girl)—repulsive and lost his consciousness in sheer panic. He also found the *bhairavi*'s erotic songs designed to please Ramakrishna quite troubling, though he once sucked her breasts in the *bhava* of a child.[8]

The report of Ramakrishna's *tantra sadhana* with Yogeshwari alarmed his young wife, as I've mentioned, and she rushed to Kamarpukur, to be near her husband and most probably to protect him from the influence of this adult female.[9] Here, as a young adolescent girl, she became close to her husband for the first time and met with an unexpected disappointment.

Ramakrishna avoided any husbandly relationship with his wife because of his ascetic aversion to women and wealth *(kamini-kanchana)*. He taught his young wife about the unreality of the world and its trials and tribulations, and once said to her: "Detachment and devotion are the only things that matter. What would one gain by bearing children, like bitches and vixens?"[10] He even tried to frighten her about the agony of motherhood if the children died.[11] When, after repeated allusions to deaths of children, Sarada protested, "Will all of them really die?," the exasperated ascetic yelled: "Ah me! Here indeed I have trampled on the tail of a deadly snake. Dear me! I thought she was nice and innocent, but she seems to know a lot!"[12] She also remembered how her celibate husband was upset with a devotee who had dared to suggest that offspring were necessary for performing the last rites over their parents' corpses. "What, to procreate children for the sake of this body?" Ramakrishna exclaimed, began spitting on the floor, and drifted into samadhi.[13]

This denial of her feminine sexuality was to be the cornerstone of Sarada's unrequited love life and her initiation into an immaculate marriage with an unconventional ascetic–a thoroughgoing householder and yet reputed to be a renouncer of the world and worldliness. It is interesting to note that Ramakrishna's Vedantic teacher Ishwar Totapuri, an itinerant ascetic of the Dashnami sect who went about naked (Ramakrishna referred to him as "the naked one," *nyangta*), regarded his young Bengali disciple as "really established in Brahman." Since he manifested "self-abnegation, detachment, discrimination, and realization," the teacher declared that he could lose "no spiritual value" and "incurred no demerit" by performing "his duty towards his wife."[14] Yet Ramakrishna insisted on remaining a celibate.

Saradananda comments on Sarada's delayed physiological development, which made her look like a little girl.[15] Another biographer, Sanghaguru Matilal, observes that "it is not unreasonable to suppose that he [Ramakrishna] was saved [from carnality] because of . . . unnatural difference in age."[16] Though the young Ramakrishna is reported to have commented favorably on the appearance of his child-bride on the marriage night—"You're fine, okay"—he somehow was uncomfortable with her feminine smell, such as the pungent odor of coconut oil emanating from her hair. On the same night he refused to share his bed with her and asked her to sleep in it by herself because, as he told her, "I can't stand the smell of coconut oil."[17] Possibly Saradamani was a plain-looking young woman, though not outright homely. Even one of Saradamani's most devoted disciples of later years, Sarala Mukhopadhyay, was terribly disappointed when as an eight year-old girl she had met Sarada, who looked like an ordinary woman. The child Sarala, of course, liked her "but still wondered how she could be anything other than an ordinary woman."[18] Sarada's lack of physical beauty and attraction may be one of the reasons why her husband could detach himself effortlessly from any erotic feelings for her and remark to Golap-ma that his wife was Goddess Saraswati, who had come to this world in the guise of a homely woman with a view to sparing lustful men their well-deserved punishment for ogling a pretty female.[19] On the other hand, we have Ramakrishna's confession to sexual arousal at the sight of a near-naked, full-bodied young woman.[20]

II

Sarada's marital (and maternal) disappointments deepened in the coming years. Ramakrishna left Kamarpukur after a few months in 1867. For the next four years he stayed away from his village and began practicing various *sadhanas*. The post-*bhairavi* phase of his ascetic life was marked first by *vatsalya bhava*—that is, his spiritual state in the mood of a child spent dallying with the doll Ramalala (a brass image of the child Rama) given to him at Dakshineshwar by a roving monk with matted hair *(jata)* known as Jatadhari. The *vatsalya* state was followed by his ecstatic state, the so-called *madhura bhava*, the "sweet mood" of Radha, restive in Krishna's absence. This is the period of Ramakrishna's *dibyonmada* condition (the state of holy insanity) when he dressed and behaved like the Radha of the Bengali folklore restive in divine rut—that is, with acute lust for Krishna, an incarnation of Lord Vishnu. When rumors that the young priest had lost his head due to self-inflicted continence reached Jairambati in March 1872, Sarada, by now in her late teens, hastened to Dakshineshwar in utter panic. Her unannounced arrival at the Kali temple seemed to upset the Master and caused him great anxiety and alarm, as he had now to deal with his nineteen-year-old wife at a time when he himself had chosen to behave like a romantic Radha madly in love with the lusty Lord Krishna. All this time Sarada had been growing out of childhood at her paternal home at Jairambati.

III

We need to try to understand, in human terms, Ramakrishna's sexuality and attempt a psychological explanation. While I am aware at all times of the pitfalls of psychoanalyzing a religious personality, yet as a historian I have decided to discount the realm of the magical and the anagogical and examine the personal as well as the cultural forces and factors that might have been responsible for Ramakrishna's "celibate" marriage. My attempt is predicated on my conviction that Ramakrishna's psychic experiences were conditioned by normal human motives.[21] Ramakrishna, it would seem from the available sources, was androgynous from the time of his childhood.[22] He was quite a prankster, but never a rowdy *boy*. Somewhat effeminate and quite used to the company of women, he, reportedly felt no reaction whatsoever when he peeked at the naked women bathing in the village pond. In fact, he grew to be an accomplished entertainer of the women of the community and an intimate companion of the village belles.[23] In the household of a local worthy, Sitanath Pyne, as well as in that of many others in the traders' quarters, the women became extremely fond of the boy Gadadhar and treated him like the child Krishna (Gopala), especially for his impersonation of various mythological characters and for his ecstatic trances, to which he was quite prone.[24]

Ramakrishna's disciple-biographer Saradananda reports that Gadadhar in his adolescent years used to be afflicted with a desire to be a woman because he felt jealous of the *gopis* (cow girls) of Braja, who as females earned the privilege of enjoying Lord Krishna's intimacy. He despaired of his male physique and wished to be a woman—in particular, a child-widow, who would carry out the household chores and spin yarns while singing songs dedicated to Krishna during the day and after sundown would weep with a longing to feed Krishna sweets made with his own hands; then he would be blessed when the Lord would materialize as a cowherd boy to partake of the offerings.[25]

Physically, Ramakrishna exhibited some feminine features. Saradananda writes that the Master's body became as tender as that of a child or a woman as a consequence of his prolonged ecstatic state.[26] One can very well see from the extant photographs of Ramakrishna that he possessed quite well-formed and firm breasts—possibly a case of gynecomastia. Vivekananda's brother Mahendranath Datta has observed: "It happens sometimes that a man harbors both male and female features—beard as well as breasts—in the same body."[27] Datta must have had Ramakrishna in mind. SriM (Mahendranath Gupta) noted how one day the ecstatic Master held a pillow to his breast as if he were nursing an infant.[28] Ramakrishna himself quite unabashedly described his feminine behavior and attitude. Once he sat after a midday siesta with his loincloth disheveled. He then remarked that he was sitting like a woman about to suckle her baby.[29] In fact, he used to suckle his beloved young disciple Rakhal Ghosh (later Swami Brahmananda). "What a beautiful childlike nature Rakhal has!" Ramakrishna observed while recalling his days with the boy. "While at play, he would come running to me, sit on my lap, and suck my tits" *(Rakhaler ki sundar balakbhav, khelte khelte doude ese amar kole base mai khai).*[30]

Ramakrishna's assumed femininity was at times so intense and sincere that he seems to have exhibited the classic behavioral syndrome of a transsexual imagining having feminine physiological functions.[31] Saradananda writes about Ramakrishna's fantastic bleeding "from every pore of his body" as result of his "extreme anguish of the heart." The Master attained that state having been oblivious of his own body in deep contemplation of Radha. He became, Saradananda goes on, so obsessed with the thought of regarding himself as a woman that he would see himself as a female even in dreams.[32] Ramakrishna even claimed to have experienced menstruation (bleeding from his *swadhisthanachakra*, region around his pubic hair), and the bleeding continued for three days, just like the menstrual period of women.[33]

In psychological terms, Ramakrishna exhibited an attitude of *paraphilia*—"an erotosexual syndrome in which a person is reiteratively responsive to and dependent on atypical . . . stimulus imagery, in fantasy or in practice. . . ."[34] *Paraphilia* stems from a gender-identity/role disorder in which "there is ambivalence, confusion, or male/female transposition relative to one's personal sense of masculinity or femininity" resulting in the development of a "feminine obligatory" personality betraying his gender-identity/role status "in his speech, gait, and often exaggerated feminine mannerisms and etiquette."[35] We have Ramakrishna's confession of his inexplicable (to him) failure to develop as a normal male. Once he lamented: "I desired so much to marry, to be able to visit my in-laws' home, have lots of fun [in life]! But, alas, [I don't know] what happened to me!"[36]

IV

Gadadhar's cross-gender confusion might have been the outcome of his identity confusion, which subsequently resulted in his "delayed or prolonged adolescence." Psychologists ascribe identity confusion to "a severe sexual traumatization in childhood."[37] I speculate with Jeffrey Masson that Ramakrishna had suffered some real trauma, most probably sexual seduction, which might explain his adult paranoia about female sexuality.[38] Accounts of Ramakrishna's reported behavior and conversations suggest another psychic problem. Quite possibly he was what R. D. Laing has called an "ontologically insecure individual, who cannot take the realness, aliveness, autonomy, and identity of himself and others for granted" and thus contrives ways and means to preserve his identity, his self. Such a person tends to experience himself primarily as split into a mind and a body. This split between self and body "deprives the unembodied self from direct participation in any aspect of the life of the world."[39] Ramakrishna habitually

referred to himself in the third person as "this one" (*eite* or *eta*), by pointing to his body, as if his self was apart from his body. Growing up with a
disjunction of his inner self and his outer personality, Ramakrishna found
safety and reassurance in not being himself. Thus, all through his childhood and even during his adult years he played feminine parts. He also
considered mimesis, or the technique of what the Vaishnavas would call
raganuga, extremely important for spiritual purposes. He once advised a
young visitor from Agarpara, a northern suburb of Calcutta: "A man's character can change through *aropa* [imposition or imitation]. Lust can be de-
stroyed by imitating *prakriti*. Genuine feminine behavior can thus be
acquired."[40]

V

Ramakrishna also harbored quite an idiosyncratic notion of human sexuality. He insisted that the best way for a man to conquer lust is to behave
like a woman.[41] Curiously enough, he endorsed and even encouraged heterosexual female passion, while he was fearful and disdainful of heterosexual male passion. He harbored a pathological hatred and fear of
heterosexual contact or thought. "If my body is touched by a woman I feel
sick," he confessed to Dr. Mahendralal Sarkar, his physician. "The touched
part aches as if stung by a horned catfish *(singimachh)*."[42] Here we must
recall that a traumatic childhood might have resulted in "bisexual confusion." A solution to this problem is, according to Erikson, "an ascetic turning away from sexuality."[43] Ramakrishna's ascetic solution or *Seelenwollust*
(soul voluptuousness) was a feminine surrender to God.

His upbringing in a Vaishnava household and society facilitated his
"unmanning" by simulating a passive feminine behavior and by allowing
him to imagine himself to be a woman in divinely lusty liaison with the
great lover-god Krishna. Ramakrishna unabashedly revealed his eroticism—
in psychiatric terms, cacodemonomania—in respect of this god whom he
came to worship in the attitude of a lover (in the Vaishnavic lexicon, *madhura
bhava*). To him, sexuality liberated from conventional heterosexual relationships was immaculate. The famous seventeenth-century Vaishnava
scholar Vishwanath Chakravarti had enjoined the male devotees to imitate
such divine models as Radha or the *gopis* (cow girls) only with "the medi-
tative perfected body." Physical imitation with the *sadhaka*'s actual body
had to refer not to the divine but to the paradigmatic imitators of the divine
model. In other words, for a Vaishnava it was not necessary to behave like
a real Radha or a real *gopi* (presuming, of course, their historicity), but to
behave like the Vaishnava masters of the past such as Chaitanya or Rupa

Goswami, who were the spiritual models. Ramakrishna did imitate Chaitanya but did not rest there. He actually sought to *become* woman in his grand act of mimesis.[44]

While lecturing on the various Vaishnava *bhavas* (moods or states), he referred to the "*Shanta*, the serene, attitude of the ascetics," which he likened to "the wife's single-minded devotion to her husband. She knows, 'My husband is Kandarpa'." Kandarpa or Madana, incidentally, is the Hindu god of sex. Ramakrishna's preferred *bhava* was *madhura*, which he defined as "the attitude of Shrimati, that is, Radha."[45] He of course said that the "*gopis* [cow girls; Radha was a *gopi*] did not experience lust," presumably because they made love to Krishna, who was God. The implication is that love for God is lustless or immaculate, even though it is not clear whether love or lust for God generates erotic sentiments.[46] Actually it did, as could be gathered from his conversations. "Intercourse with a woman!" Ramakrishna shuddered at the idea. "What pleasure is there in that? The realization of God brings million-fold happiness." However, his description of this divine euphoria or *Seligkeit* was couched in an extremely erotic language. As he explained to Pandit Gaurikanta Tarkabhusan of Indesh (a village in Bankura): "With the attainment of *mahabhava* or divine ecstasy all the pores of the body, even the roots of the hair, become one super vagina–*mahayoni*, and in every pore one feels the pleasure of intercourse with the *atman*."[47] This is the classic tantric sexual metaphor that describes sexual embrace "as if each pore of the skin were a vulva and intercourse were taking place over the whole body. . . ." This constitutes the supreme bliss for a *sadhaka* and, minus the "mystical balderdash," *ananda* is "pure and simple pleasure of the intercourse."[48]

VI

As a young man, Ramakrishna reacted pathetically at the insinuation of sex. During the period of his so-called divine madness, his nephew Hriday procured a prostitute in order to entice his uncle from the path of divine love to carnal lust. When the patient sighted the temptress, he was overtaken with mortal fear of being stung by a poisonous snake.[49] When Ramakrishna's employers, the proprietors of the Dakshineswar Kali temple—namely, Rani Rasmani and her son-in-law and temple manager Mathuramohan Biswas—tried to relieve the high-strung young priest of his self-inflicted austerity and took him to a brothel in north Calcutta, Ramakrishna almost died at the sight of the whores. He lost consciousness, and his genitals contracted and recoiled into his crotch "like the limbs of a tortoise."[50] Even a most provocatively erotic pose of a young woman in the

Navarasika (name of a Kartabhaja sect) hangout at Kachibagan, near Calcutta, where he went in the company of a Kartabhaja named Pandit Vaishnavacharan, failed to arouse Ramakrishna. She had taken his big toe into her mouth. It is tantalizingly suggestive of an act of fellatio, though not quite this act. He seemed to have remained impervious to the provocation by another woman who made "a very ugly gesture" *(ati kutsit bhab),* but he was terribly upset.[51]

An anonymous crazy woman *(pagli)*—who, though not quite clinically insane, could be described, like Ramakrishna, as divinely mad—often visited Dakshineshwar. Most probably she had a crush on the young priest of the Kali temple. Upon questioning her why she was shedding tears one day she confessed that she harbored a *madhura bhava* toward him but felt that he was neglecting her. As Swami Gambhirananda reports, Ramakrishna was so upset on being propositioned that he jumped up from his seat instantaneously, his *dhoti* (loincloth) dropped off, and he began parading up and down the room like a raving lunatic, hurling strong curse words at the unsuspecting woman.[52] In fact, his strategy to drive women out of his sight was to get naked. Sarada recalled how the women of Kamarhati used to gawk at her handsome husband. The latter requested his companion Hriday to cover his (Ramakrishna's) face with a veil quickly and threatened that otherwise he would strip off his clothes. When warned by Hriday that his purposive nudity would raise people's eyebrows, Ramakrishna explained that this was his way of getting rid of women.[53]

VII

There may be several explanations for such an attitude. But we need to discount a devotee's belief that Ramakrishna's celibate life was based upon his mother's admonition to him, after he had been caught peeking at women bathing in the village pond, to behave like a son to all women in the village.[54] Apparently his gynephobia caused his ascetic aversion for *kamini-kanchana* ("woman and gold," that is, "lust and lure")—a phrase that became a leitmotif in his sermons and teachings—which might be interpreted psychologically as the "ascetic escape" from anxiety.[55] According to one writer, "[T]his attitude in part reflects Ramakrishna's high caste background, in which the social separation of the sexes is the norm."[56] We must, however, remember that as an adolescent Gadadhar delighted in the company of women. And he loved female company, one suspects, because he felt not as a man among women but *as one of them.*

Another explanation has it that the figure of woman and gold, that is, *kamini-kanchana,* "signified a social world of everyday transactions in which the family man was held in bondage." Ramakrishna's admonition against this bondage sought to guide the Hindu male to his culturally sanctioned goal—*mukti* (liberation). The male essence *(purusa)* represented the principle of stasis or rest, whereas the female essence *(prakriti)* represented change unleashing the forces of desire *(pravritti),* thereby bringing about degeneration and death in the male.[57] Indeed, Ramakrishna's recommended book to his young devotees was the *Mukti ebam Tahar Sadhan,* which, inter alia, cited Shankaracharya's *Maniratnamala,* which counseled men seeking liberation to give up women because they are the devil incarnate. The *Mukti* extolled the efficacy of the celibate *(urdhareta).*[58] Ramakrishna's conviction in the efficacy of *enkrateia* or continence was so deep that he enjoined his disciples to practice it for the sake of understanding spiritual sermons adequately. He told his friend Mahimacharan Chakravarti that "without controlling the discharge of semen, one simply cannot comprehend all this" [sermons].[59]

This obsession with control is part of what Philip Spratt calls the "narcissistic psyche" of the Hindus who generally believe that "a man who possesses a store of . . . good semen becomes a superman."[60] The *Manusmriti* categorically explicates a kind of "sexual and moral hydrostatics" by proclaiming that any uncontrolled organ of the male causes his loss of wisdom just like water flowing out of a water carrier's skin bag through one hole.[61] Patanjali and the classical yoga speaks of *ojas,* "a sort of hierogenetic power residing in, or embodied by[,] the semen which has not been shed."[62] Masson observed that the "sexual fantasies of immense prowess are of course only the other side of the coin from constant fears of sexual depletion."[63] Thus the conquest of carnality is a primary condition for spiritual realization. Hence Ramakrishna's *sadhana* (spiritual exercise) to conquer lust. Hence also his reluctance to act the part of an active husband to his young wife.

Ramakrishna's virility anxiety leading to his aversion to sex might have been caused as much by his own idea about immaculate sex as by the physical infirmities that had afflicted him since his youth. We do have at least one telltale indication that he might have suffered from involuntary discharge of semen even when awake–most probably a case of spermatorrhoea *(jiryan).* Saradananda reports that once Ramakrishna "saw a worm going out of [his] body with the urine." Terribly distraught, he told his employer Mathuramohan "with a sad face" what he had seen and was reassured by the latter that it was a "lust-worm" that had left his body "by the grace of the Mother [Kali]."[64] When Ramakrishna attempted (for the first and the last time) to make love to his teenage wife and stretched out his arms to embrace her, "within the flash of a moment someone drained him of his libido [*jibaner bidyutshakti*, literally meaning, "electric energy of life"] and he completely lost his consciousness."[65] This appears to be a spiritual explanation for what in fact is a simple physiological disorder such as premature ejaculation. My supposition seems to be confirmed by Ramakrishna's own admission. When his friend the Brahmo scholar Shivanath Shastri (1847–1919) charged him with inflicting a "virtual widowhood" on his young wife, the Master confessed: "Why do you complain? It is no longer possible, it is all dead and gone."[66]

VIII

Most probably, Ramakrishna's contempt for women was the defense mechanism of an insecure male, who thought of himself as a woman in order to fight his innate fear of the female. "I am terribly scared of women," he confessed candidly. "I see them as a tigress coming to devour me. Besides, I see large pores in their limbs. I find all of them to be ogres." He recalled how a landlord from Ulogram village remarked on seeing Ramakrishna's ecstatic state that "the goddess has gripped him, like a tiger grabbing a man" and added: "I was young then, quite plump and always in ecstasy."[67] Ramakrishna's vision of woman possessing large holes all over her body was most certainly his exaggerated fear of the vagina. The memory of his frequent childhood encounters with the women of Kamarpukur might have suggested to him the reason for their infatuation with a cuddly ecstatic boy.

Indeed, what the women of Kamarpukur did to the young boy by teasing him as their Krishna while pretending to be his *gopis* is far from clear. It is quite reasonable to speculate that these experiences led him to consider women as voluptuous and immoral. We do have a clear reference to his suspicion of female enticement even under the guise of motherly behavior. He once reported:

> Haripada [a young devotee] has come under the spell of a slut [*magi*] from Ghoshpara. She puts on an affectionate attitude toward him; but Haripada is a mere boy and doesn't understand anything. Women like her behave that way whenever they spot young boys. I heard that Haripada even lies on her lap and she feeds him with her own hands. I shall warn him that this is not good. That very filial affection will lead to undesirable feelings. These women practice spiritual discipline with men; they regard men as Krishna. They call men "Lover Krishna."

He reiterated the point at another time: "Many women ensnare good-looking young men. Hence their 'attitude of Gopala'."[68] The fear and suspicion of female seduction of his adult life must have been caused by the unconscious trauma of his childhood as well as by his later experience with the

Bhairavi Yogeshwari, who used to make him sit on her lap and feed him with her own hands.

Such experiences might have induced a mixed reaction in him: pleasant and yet repulsive. He was especially curious about and even quite conscious of the female body. We have noted his childhood voyeurism earlier. Even after he had become a *paramahamsa* and earned reputation as a supreme renunciant, he revealed his knowledge of the sexual attractions of a full-figured female. His monastic biographer Saradananda reports in guarded language that the Master considered the shape of female breasts ("that particular organ with the help of which women acquire the glory of motherhood") as indicator of female animality. Also women possessed of heavy hips ("those whose buttocks bulge out like black ants" [*pashchatbhag pipilikar nyay uccha*]) are particularly lascivious.[69] As a young man he seems to have been troubled by this ambivalence. Satyacharan Mitra writes about Ramakrishna's feeling of lust on staring at the curves of a full-figured young woman on the bank of the Ganges in a wet sari through which "the beauty of her body had become acutely accentuated" *(soundaryer prakharata bardhita)* and then his bolting like a crazy man and praying to Kali to calm himself down.[70] Hence he contemptuously described the female body as nothing but "such things as blood, flesh, entrails, worms, piss, shit, and the like"[71] and insisted on disciplining, even discarding, if need be, intransigent spouses with their multiple mundane demands who kept their husbands away from spiritual company. "Discard your wife," the Master thundered, "if she creates an obstacle in the way of God. Let her even kill herself or do whatever she can."[72]

As a matter of fact, Ramakrishna's attitude to women in general contained a streak of misogyny. He is reported to have told his nephew Hridayram that women are generally untrustworthy (that is, they cheat on their menfolk) and hence they ought to be kept busy at all times. "One must not trust that race [of women]. Women ought to cook only. . . . Only cooking helps them become good," the cautious uncle told his nephew.[73] The target of this obloquy was none other than his own wife, Sarada, and his niece Lakshmimani the widow, who he feared would stare at men [all the time] if they were not kept busy. Indeed, the master believed that cooking helps stabilize women's minds *(mon bhalo thake)*. He told his niece Lakshmi that Sita, Draupadi, and the goddesses Lakshmi and Parvati all were deft and diligent cooks.[74] He was so concerned for the sexual safety of his young wife after his death that he strictly admonished her against accepting any help from or staying with any of his devotees after his death. He warned her against abandoning her Kamarpukur home even if she was invited to stay with the devotees. Accepting help from others would entail returning their favors, and thus she would be better off staying put in her village home, eating the greens she would grow in her yard with rice *(shakbhat khabe)* and singing the Lord's name.[75] He also wanted to caution her against village gossip, especially that of the women who pried into his movements and behavior and spread the canard that he did not share his wife's bed at night. He particularly warned her against taking anybody's counsel about getting her husband treated for his indifference to his wife, insisting that he possessed "everything" but that all was dedicated to God.[76] His attitude toward and degree of trust in his wife was manifest in his advice to his householder devotees: "Never trust your wife even if she is devoted to God [*bhaktimati*]."[77] He also preached: "Never trust a woman even if she rolls on the floor weeping in devotion."[78] He made his point about the inexorable immoral influence of women in his characteristic metaphor: "No matter how much care you take in the room of collyrium [*kajal*, standing for women, who use it as eyeliner], you can't avoid being stained a little."[79]

Ramakrishna's contempt for women as an impediment to the spiritual realization of the male reflects a deep-seated anxiety typical of high-caste Hindus. In order to explain this anxiety, we need to have some idea of the split mother-image of the Hindu woman, whose unrequited sexual expectations are sublimated into her close and erotically charged relationship with the son. When the child grows up and is detached from the physical closeness of his mother, he develops an anxiety that creates an image of his mother as cruel and capricious (who is perceived as arbitrarily withdrawing affection with the birth of subsequent siblings and thus punishing him). This image of the bad mother is related psychically to the growing son's anxiety and fear of maternal incest. And when the child finally develops into an adult, he harbors a fear of a sexually mature woman, even though he regards her as an object of sexual gratification. His fear and anxiety are resolved when the wife turns into "a safe mother who, frustrated in her sexual dealings with her husband, transfers such feelings to the newborn son, thus perpetuating the syndrome."[80] A byproduct of this psychosocial situation is the culturally sanctioned sanctimonious contempt for the woman who is feared for her insatiable sexual appetite and her threat to male virility. The woman is thus at once an object of sexual desire and an instrument of perpetuating the family line and an object of sexual fear and anxiety "generated by maternal incest danger, which may in turn create negative feelings towards women."[81]

Lakshmi-didi (Lakshmimani Ghatak, 1864-1926)

4

Saradamani as *Parmahamsa*'s Wife and Widow: The Making of the Divine Mother

> The Unique divine Incarnation that he [Ramakrishna] was, had to set an ideal for householders and Sannyasins alike. This was achieved by his association with Sarada Devi, who in later times distinguished herself in being a wife, a nun and a mother at the same time.
>
> —Tapasyananda, *Sri Ramakrishna*

I

Ramakrishna's solution to his personal problem (in respect of his continence as a married man) came through his young and unsuspecting wife evolving into a *devi*. At Kamarpukur in 1867 he had assumed her mother's role, teaching her manners and morals. Now he made her believe that *she* was the mother, indeed the Divine Mother, or to quote his exact words, "Ma Anandamayi,"[1] though in reality, Sarada was constantly tormented by the jealous Bhariavi (Yogeshwari), who could not stomach her newfound disciple spending time with his young wife.[2] Ramakrishna had already convinced Bhanu *pisi* (Aunt Bhanu)—no relation to Sarada, but a friend of her family—that he was Shiva and Sarada Shiva's consort.[3] At another time he proclaimed her to be his Shakti and, as has been noted earlier, Saraswati, simply because "Sarada" appears to be another appellation of the goddess.[4] And at another time he quipped: "Do you think I have married a mere veggie [*laushak- khaki, puishak-khaki*]?"[5] He effortlessly appointed his illiterate but totally loyal devotee, the Bihari boy Latu (formerly a manservant at the home of Ramakrishna's householder disciple Ramchandra Datta and later Swami Adbhutananda), as Sarada's factotum, telling him that she was in fact the goddess of his meditation.[6]

He must have succeeded eminently in deifying Saradamani and thus rendering her sexually irrelevant and innocuous. As he deposed later, he had anxiously prayed to the goddess Kali to wipe out all erotic feelings from her mind. He felt safe when he actually came in contact with her during March 1872–October 1873 and knew that his prayers to the goddess had been answered.[7] And yet it must be noted that Ramakrishna did not think that Sarada was advanced enough to be considered a liberated soul *(jibanmukta)*. Sister Nivedita (Margaret Noble) wrote to her friend Josephine MacLeod that Loki-didi (meaning Lakshmi-didi, that is, Lakshmimani, Ramakrishna's niece) had told her "the other night how Sri Ramakrishna had said of *her* (not the Holy Mother, but L. D.) that she is already on the other side—a jivanmukta—and she has never known either joy or sorrow."[8]

II

Sarada's divine status was recognized and legitimized through a number of painful and powerful experiences and by a variety of agents ranging from her ecstatic husband to a penitent highwayman. Nikhilananda documents a number of events in her life from 1872 through Ramakrishna's death in 1886 and concludes that "all this time the chrysalis was being transformed into a butterfly."[9] The most celebrated of these events is, of course, the *kumari puja* (virgin worship, supposedly a tantric ritual) or the *sodashi puja* (worship of the sixteen-year-old) celebrated by her husband, who actually worshiped her as a goddess on 25 May 1872, the day of *phalaharini* (destroyer of the effects of bad karma) Kalipuja. The Master probably aimed at sealing, permanently, any prospect of his wife's ever making a sexual overture toward him and at the same time gaining recognition as an adept who had successfully graduated in the highest tantric practices.[10] Most probably he tried to imitate his mentor Gaurikanta Tarkabhusana, who had, reportedly, worshiped his wife with flowers, believing her to be goddess Bhagavati in human form.[11]

Ramakrishna's chanting preparatory to the worship instilled most probably a feeling of alarm and vulnerability in the naive Sarada, and she was in an almost comatose state. Thus began the ritual by her saintly consort, who first invoked the power of the eternal virgin, the goddess Tripura Sundari.[12] Thereafter he performed the ritual worship of his wife and fed her some sweets with his own hand. Gambhirananda writes fervently how both Ramakrishna and Sarada gradually lost their consciousness and how "the Deity and the devotee became identified."[13] It was a strange consummation of a strange relationship! It would henceforth have nothing to do with those anxieties one associates with youth or normal heterosexual instinct. Both were dehumanized and by the same token deified.

There is an uncanny parallel between Ramakrishna's ritual deification of his wife and the ritual murder of Catherine, the wife of Charles Brown's fictional character Wieland. Just as Ramakrishna established his adept status by sacrificing or castrating his wife symbolically, so Wieland was "raised to heights of religious rapture." As Wieland is made to say after having committed the murder:

> This was a moment of triumph. Thus had I successfully subdued the stubbornness of human passions; the victim which had been demanded was given; the deed was done and past recall. I lifted the corpse in my arms and laid it on the bed. I gazed upon it with delight. Such was the elation of my thoughts, that I even broke into laughter. I clapped my hands and exclaimed, "It is done! My sacred duty is fulfilled! To that I have sacrificed, O my God! Thy last and best gift, my wife."[14]

III

Sarada's ritual deification was further affirmed by her experiences during moments of facing possible death. Sometime in 1875 she was stricken with dysentery at Dakshineshwar, and she returned to Jairambati to recover.[15] But she had a relapse that was life-threatening. When her condition deteriorated, Sarada decided to fast and picket before the image of Simhavahini (Lion-borne, another appellation of the goddess Jagaddhatri, "Upholder of the Universe," that is, "Mother of the Universe") until the goddess relented and prescribed a cure. A cure was in fact suggested to her in a dream, and she ultimately recovered. The goddess, however, told Sarada in another dream that she had no time for any other human being than her. Sarada was so convinced of her intimacy with Lion-borne that she "always kept with her a little earth from the temple grounds and used to eat one or two grains of it daily."[16] This divine liaison must have toughened Sarada to endure the ordeals of other pathological experiences such as her coping successfully with an onslaught of malaria accompanied by enlargement of the spleen. She even patiently went through the cruel treatment of having her abdomen branded with the lighted branch of a palm tree. And she was cured!

Subsequent episodes further confirmed her divine liaison and even divine identity. Sometime in late 1876, at Jairambati, she dreamed that the goddess Jagaddhatri asked to be worshiped a second time (the first worship had been performed by Sarada's mother, Shyamasundari, the previous year, following a similar dream). The goddess thus importuned Sarada, who had refused to accede to her mother's request to contribute toward an annual worship of the goddess, as she was too indigent herself to contribute anything but physical labor.[17] In February 1877, on the way from her parental

home to Dakshineshwar, Sarada encountered a low-caste *(bagdi)* brigand
who recognized her as the goddess Kali, and she fondly addressed him as
her "robber-father" *(dakat-baba)*.[18] One of the *paramahamsa*'s earliest devotees to worship Sarada as the goddess Bhagavati was his *rasaddar,* Shambhu
Mullick's wife.[19]

IV

In spite of her being treated as a goddess by Ramakrishna, Sarada remained an all-suffering, demure village woman at the beck and call of her
ecstatic husband. The caste-conscious and comfort-seeking renouncer of
kamini-kanchana converted his wife into a domestic hand who catered to
his creature comforts, especially his demands for good food daily. It is as if
he had procured a housemaid through the culturally sanctioned ritual of
Hindu marriage. There is an ironical truth in Swami Nirvedananda's observation that "Ramakrishna's behaviour towards his wife . . . beats all records.
It is strange, unprecedented and obviously beyond the range of human understanding. "[20] In fact, Sarada's entire young adult life was spent cooking
for and catering to her husband and his admirers. Reportedly she used to
enter into the *nahabat* (a small room adjoining the temple at Dakshineshwar
used originally for the hired performers of a pipe instrument called *shanai,*
played on the occasion of various religious festivals) regularly at three in
the morning and could never come out even for the purpose of answering
calls of nature. On her own admission: "Then at times it so happened that I
could finish today's toilet tomorrow only" *(takhan takhan emono hoyechhe
ye ajker haga kal hegechhi)*.[21] When once she had to leave Dakshineshwar
for Kamarpukur to attend a wedding, Ramakrishna bemoaned his plight to
his devotees.[22]

Though reputed to be an ascetic renunciant with the honorific appellation of *paramahamsa*, Ramakrishna in fact was extremely fond of creature
comforts, especially food.[23] His food fetish was truly phenomenal. Sarada
relates that the first thing her husband would talk about early in the morning was what he would like to eat during lunch. She usually followed his
elaborate instructions on the menu scrupulously, and she would be upset if
she could not find the specific spices that he would like her to use in cooking that day. Once she could not find the particular spice that the
paramahamsa had asked her to use for cooking the *dal* (lentil soup), but he
insisted that she cook with that particular spice. The angry gourmet or-
dered her to get it from the village shop. He was piqued by the fact that, as
he declared, he had left the rich fare of the Dakshineshwar temple for the
sake of a simple meal at home, which he now found hard to get.[24]

Even though he was extremely fond of spicy food—"Season your lentil soup in such a way that it will make a hog grunt,"[25] he would say—he was constitutionally unable to put up with all kinds of foods. His wife knew what aliments would suit him. He had a weak stomach, and he could not eat the foods prepared in the kitchen of Dakshineshwar Temple, even though he had boasted of the temple food and favorably compared it to Sarada's cooking. When one day she declined to cook because she had her period—a time considered unclean in Hindu society—Ramakrishna posited his own thesis that there is nothing wrong about a menstruating woman cooking food, just as there is nothing inherently impure about human body, the purity-impurity binary being a matter of thought and perception.[26]

This bit of sermon flatly contradicted the Master's contempt for the female body with its entrails, flesh, bones, filth, shit, blood, and the like.[27] Even when terminally ill at Kashipore, Calcutta, the Master would be concerned for his foods. He was prescribed a special diet of boiled cream of wheat and rice mixed with meat and clam stew. When asked to prepare the clam stew, Sarada refused to slaughter clams. This threw the patient into a fit of rage, and she ultimately decided to comply. Once again, this behavior of the dying man went against his admonition to one of his young devotees some years earlier that "a man of realisation can never be cruel to others. It is against his very nature."[28]

Ramakrishna's favorite daily meal at dinnertime was *luchi* (fried bread) and farina pudding.[29] His favorite snack was sweet cream or *sar*.[30] He was very careful about bad breath. He always carried with him a small pouch containing such mouth refreshers as aniseed, cardamom, cloves, caraway seed, and cubeb *(kababchini)*.[31] He counseled SriM to clean his tongue regularly, presumably because he felt negatively about the devotee's morning breath.[32] He advised his devotee Gangadhar Ghatak (later Swami Akhandananda) to chew *pan* to freshen up his postprandial breath.[33] His usual diversion after a meal consisted in body (chiefly feet) massage by his devotees, most often SriM, who even felt that "the Master was actually teaching him how to serve [God or a God-man]."[34]

Though Ramakrishna provided an explanation for his eating habits by citing from the *Bhagavad Gita* that "the *jnani* himself does not eat but makes offerings to his *kundalini* while appearing to eat," this statement cannot be located in the *Gita*, which, however, clearly states that "gluttons have no discipline, nor the man who starves himself , nor he who sleeps excessively or suffers wakefulness." From the *Gita*'s point of view, the Master was neither a *stithaprajna,* a man of perfect equipoise, nor a yogi "moderate in his eating and his recreation."[35] Ramakrishna's other explanation for his culinary cravings makes a better sense. "Why do I eat a variety of dishes?" he asked, and answered himself: "Monotonous meals might compel me to

give up [my ministry]."[36] Food seems to have provided the mad lover of
God with the fuel for his colorful ecstasies and enstasis. It might also have
provided him with the psychic strength to combat the stress that might
have afflicted the renouncer of *kamini-kanchana*.

Saradamani's constant companion Yogen-Ma (Yogindramohini Biswas)
provides a graphic description of the Holy Mother's service to her husband
during mealtimes. Sarada would finish her bath before sunrise, perform her
daily meditation, and then begin her cooking under the staircase of the
nahabat at Dakshineshwar, where she slept all by herself. After finishing
the cooking, she would massage her husband's body with oil, thus preparing him for his bath. During his bath she would prepare betel rolls *(pan)*.
He would come for the meal about eleven and perch on a small carpet
(asan) spread by her. She would also keep a glass of water for him by the
side and bring his food. While he ate she would keep on conversing with
him but would take care not so say anything that would induce a spiritual
emotion inducing samadhi and thereby spoiling his meal. After his eating
was over, she would hand him some betel rolls and the glass of water. She
would partake some of the leavings from her husband's plate *(prasada)* and
then sing a song in a low tone for his postprandial entertainment.[37]

V

Apparently the Kali temple at Dakshineshwar was a veritable haven of
bliss, *ananda niketan*, as it were. The *nahabat* was used by the *shanai* play-
ers to perform throughout the day, from the early hours of the morning to
the evening. Scores of devotees and traveling mendicants visited the place
every day.[38] Ramakrishna lived in this charming and serene atmosphere in
superb comfort—singing, dancing, eating good food, and being ecstatic to
everybody's wonderment. "This world is a load of fun. I eat (and drink) and
make merry" *(ei samsar majar kuti, ami khai dai ar maja luti)*—he loved
to repeat this doggerel often.[39] He frankly told Krishnakishore Bhattacharya:
"It's my sweet pleasure to chew betel-leaf, look at my face in the mirror,
and dance naked among a thousand girls."[40]

Only Saradamani never got to be a part of the spiritual court presided
over by her husband, the princely renunciant. She remained on the margins
of this male-dominated world of food and fun. From Nikhilananda's biography we come to know that Sarada slept without a mattress on a simple
mat and a pillow stuffed with jute fibers left over from the slings that she
had to make to hang pots of sweets for her husband's visitors. She must
have been greatly relieved when her bedstead improved later.[41] Nikhilananda

Yogen-ma (Yogindramohini Biswas, 1851–1924)

describes her spartan abode in the *nahabat*. It was actually a stuffy room with a floor space of fifty square feet and nine-foot-high ceiling. Often a couple of Ramakrishna's women devotees shared this room during overnight stay. A pot of water containing live fish hung from the ceiling. The fish were meant for the Master's meal, but they splashed water all over the floor.[42] Ramakrishna was reputed to be a strict disciplinarian and hence would never allow his overworked wife to sleep longer than what he considered adequate. Reportedly he would pour water on her bed if she overslept.[43] After one has read Nikhilananda's saga of the mute tribulations of the hapless Holy Mother, one cannot but appreciate the remark made by a visitor to Sarada's room: "She is in exile, as it were, like Sita."[44]

The saint seems to have squandered all his humanity and love on others, especially on his devotees and admirers, and not much was left for his own wife. When the wife of his patron Balaram Basu fell ill, Sarada was instructed by her husband to visit the patient. Though Balaram's home was some five miles away from Dakshineshwar, she could have undertaken the journey by foot, as she was used to walking long distances. However, part of the way ran through the city, and she, like most women of her day, felt uneasy about being seen publicly. She therefore asked for a conveyance. Ramakrishna snapped back: "What! You won't go when my Balaram's family is facing disaster? You'll walk; go on foot."[45] She submitted to his demands, though mercifully she was provided with a conveyance by a kindhearted devotee. Yet she unhesitatingly declared that she suffered no discomfort if she did anything for his service.[46]

VI

An unlettered and unsophisticated woman from rural Bengal, Sarada was so thoroughly influenced by her husband's various injunctions and insinuations that she considered herself especially fortunate because he never addressed her with the familiar *tui* (Bengali for the Hindi *tu*). "Ah! How he treated me! Not even once did he say to me a harsh word or wound my feelings," she proudly recalled long after his death.[47] However, as noted earlier, her husband harbored an anxiety about her fidelity. Quite naturally, she was advised to remain "mild and weak . . . meek and sober" by her husband, who maintained that women's strength lay in their modesty, "otherwise there will be public scandal."[48] Nevertheless, to others, the Master made it quite clear that she was divine (wife of a God-man). With a view to exploiting the services of his devotees to assist his wife in her slavish chores, Ramakrishna devised an ingenious strategy. We follow Nikhilananda here. One day while Sarada was making dough for cooking *chapati* (unleavened bread) and Latu was meditating by the riverbank, Ramakrishna told the Latu to do something more substantial—help out a real-life goddess in kneading the dough. He then took the Bihari boy to the *nahabat* and told his wife to make him do some of her chores, certifying the young man as a "pure-souled boy."[49]

That was enough. The unsuspecting Bihari, "an illustration of perfect obedience,"[50] became a part of Sarada's kitchen. In order to prevent the foul-mouthed Hriday from abusing the demure Sarada, Ramakrishna one day reminded the offender of Sarada's real identity as the Divine Mother and told him that if she was provoked, even the trinity of Brahma, Vishnu, and Maheswara could not save him from her wrath.[51]

Yet, for all his protestations of Sarada's divine status, Ramakrishna remained wonderfully impervious to any sense of guilt or remorse in respect to his wife. When accused by one of his Brahmo devotees, a university-educated young man, that he had totally neglected his wife and was advising others to leave their families, the Master first said that he had merely obeyed the dictates of Mother Kali, and then left his devotee to defecate in the garden. While squatting for evacuation he began playing with two pieces of bricks and held a "conversation" with the goddess: "Look, Ma, that son of a bitch tells me that I have done something wrong. Have I, Ma?" He then "heard" the goddess assure him that he was not guilty of anything. When he returned to his Brahmo accuser, his eyes were ablaze with spiritual fire and he told him that he did not care about what the young man had to say, because he had been told by the Divine Mother that he had done no wrong. The Brahmo devotee, reportedly, felt that Ramakrishna spoke like a god, and he became a disciple of the Master.[52]

VII

Following Ramakrishna's death on 16 August 1886, Sarada's divine reputation functioned initially as a strategy for the rehabilitation of the childless and penniless widow of the late *paramahamsa*. Sarada actually confronted a bleak prospect after her husband's death. Ramakrishna had been able to command a large following among the Calcutta *babus*, some of whom became his eager *rasaddars* (suppliers of victuals). During his lifetime Sarada had remained in the background without much personal recognition except as the Master's wife who cooked for his devotees whenever asked. Even then, as Ramakrishna's great householder disciple Ram Datta openly said after his death: "We knew *Paramahamsamashai* [Mr. Paramahamsa], but who's his wife? We do not know anything about her."[53] Swami Bhumananda has shrewdly observed that "the greatest loss following the

Master's death was sustained by Mother. In Hindu society the widow suffers the most."[54]

There indeed was a period of uncertainty when the young widow was shuffling from Cossipore to Dakshineshwar for a few days. Thereafter, probably due to the generosity of Ramakrishna's wealthy householder disciple Balaram Basu, she was dispatched to Vrindavan on a pilgrimage along with a few disciples of the Master such as Latu, Yogananda (Yogindranath Chaudhuri), and Abhedananda (Kaliprasanna Chandra), as well as some of Sarada's female devotees like Golap-ma, Yogen-ma, Krishnabhabini, Lakshimani, and Nikunjabala (SriM's wife). Upon her return, after about a year, she was the object of the curious gaze of her neighbors. The young widow's red-bordered sari and heavy gold bangles did not betray the conventional outfit of a Hindu widow but in fact looked suspiciously that of a married woman. Fearful of public censure *(loker kathar bhaye)*, Sarada took off her ornaments. Yet she remained the target of local gossip. From the villagers' point of view, she had been the widow of a city celebrity who had commanded a large following, and her neighbors could not fathom the reason of her returning to Kamarpukur to lead a lonely life of extreme hardship. Ramakrishna's employers at Dakshineshwar had initially arranged for a monthly allowance of Rs. 7.00 for the widow but later discontinued it when she was away visiting holy places.

The news of her subsistence on rice and wild plants at Kamarpukur moved her mother at Jayrambati to send for help from Calcutta. Sarada's younger brother Prasanna in fact rushed to Dakshineshwar and had a brush with the priest Ramlal, the late *paramahamsa's* nephew. On the way Prasanna also complained to Golap-ma and Yogen-ma about his sister's predicament. Both women succeeded in persuading Balaram and his wife Krishnabhavini to bring Sarada to the city under their care. They pooled support from a number of women–the wives of Girish Ghosh, Dr. Shashibhusan Ghosh, Kalipada Ghosh, SriM, and a few others, with the sole exception of Ramchandra Datta, who remained somewhat lukewarm about Ramakrishna's widow. As Bhumananda explains, some of the householder devotees *(grihibhakta)* of Ramakrishna had been so influenced by their Master's dicta against *kamini-kanchana* that they were unable to realize that the *paramahamsa's* widow was also their mother.[55] Nevertheless, most of Ramakrishna's disciples, including the influential Narendranath Datta (later Swami Vivekananda) and Girish Ghosh, the flamboyant actor and socialite of Calcutta, decided to relocate her to Calcutta to live in a rented home along with the monastic disciples of her late husband.[56]

However, Ramakrishna's renunciant disciples, who had been living in a dilapidated home at Baranagar, had no financial means to support Sarada.

These young men had absolutely no income of their own, their house rent being paid for by their householder *gurubhai*, Suresh Mitra.[57] Thus, as Bhumananda writes, "they being beggars themselves, it was quite impossible for them to pay for her rent and upkeep."[58] Sarada's village elders, especially the women of Jairambati and Kamarpukur, were uneasy about the idea of her living with the devotees of her late husband and advised her to stay with her mother or with her nephew-in-law, Ramlal. Sarada's mother, Shyamasundari, tried her best to persuade her daughter to live in her parents' home. However, on the insistence of Prasannamayi, the widowed daughter of the Laha family of Kamarpukur and a childhood friend of Gadai (Ramakrishna), Sarada was able to come to Calcutta to live with the young monks. "Why, Gadai's disciples are also like your disciple children," Prasanna counseled Sarada. "Who would care for you except them? . . . Your village people won't come to your succor in times of trouble."[59]

Ultimately the neighbors of Jairambati and Kamarpukur approved of Sarada's decision to stay in Calcutta. They felt that her association with the affluent *bhadraloks* of the city would bring some benefit to the villagers, and they hoped to be invited to Calcutta to dine on festive occasions.[60] Sarada arrived in the city sometime in May 1888 and put up with the Basus of Baghbazar until her relocation to the garden house *(baganbari)* of Nilambar Mukhopadhyay at Belur, a little village on the northern suburbs of Calcutta.[61] She also made sure that she would be cared for by her husband's boys. At her Belur residence she was visited by Narendranath, who told her that he was finding himself increasingly detached from the world. "Ma, what's happening to me?" exclaimed the ebullient young man. "I see everything is blown off from me." She was quite forthright in responding to him humorously: "Take care that you do not blow me away, too!"[62]

VIII

Sarada's reputation as a goddess received wide publicity in Calcutta. An exact chronology of this process is difficult to determine, though it is possible to chart its approximate course. According to Gambhirananda, the Jagaddhatripuja held at Jairambati on 10 November 1891 showed beyond doubt that Saradamani had been fully established in her Divine Motherhood in the heart of her intimate acquaintances.[63] In particular, her divinity was popularized and publicized by Swami Niranjanananda (Nityaniranjan Ghosh), Durgacharan Nag (Nag Mahashay), and, most notably, by Girishchandra Ghosh and Swami Vivekananda. A fearlessly outspoken individual, Niranjanananda, one of Ramkrishna's direct disciples, "preached her divinity among the devotees without any reserve."[64] When Durgacharan, a great devotee of the *paramahamsa,* came to visit Sarada at Belur sometime in 1893, he kept banging his head so hard on the steps while bowing down to his late guru's widow that the maidservant attending on the Holy Mother feared that it would bleed. The overwrought Nag paid no heed to the entreaties of Yogananda, who was in charge of Sarada's household at Belur. With a swollen forehead and in tears, crying "Ma, Ma," he was brought before her. He recovered only after she shouted Ramakrishna's name into his ears and wiped his eyes, patted his head, and fed him some fruits and sweets like a child.[65]

Girish was a habitual drinker of alcohol and smoker of hemp and a womanizer who had turned into a "born again" Hindu and a follower of Ramakrishna since his acquaintance with the Master. He confessed that he could not look at the Holy Mother, because he thought himself to be a great sinner. But when in 1891, following the death of his three-year-old son and on the suggestion of Niranjanananda, he went to Jairambati in search of consolation, he at last presented himself in front of the woman. He took a dip in a nearby pond and went to salute his Holy Mother in wet clothes. As Gambhirananda informs us, when Girish looked at Saradamani he saw in her the exact resemblance of the face of "a radiantly motherly figure" he had dreamt as a young man. He had been suffering from cholera and recovered from the deadly disease after having partaken, in dream, of some *prasada* offered by that apparition.[66]

During his stay at Jairambati, Girish one day argued vehemently with Sarada's brother Kalikumar Mukhopadhyay. He claimed that the latter's sister was truly divine and abused the skeptical brother who had refused to regard her as a goddess. The incident was more amusing than anything, and Sarada lovingly accepted the visitor's dithyrambic accolade as well as her brother's levelheaded remonstrance.[67] Several years later, in 1896, Girish created another scene at Sarada's temporary residence in Calcutta. He had come to see her off on the eve of her departure for Jairambati, and pleaded to her that she must allow him to be of service to her. With a choked voice and "face flushed with emotion," her declared her as "the Mother of the Universe—Maha-maya, Maha-Sakti" in the presence of other visitors who had gathered there.[68] Swami Saradananda, another direct disciple of Ramakrishna from a *bhadralok* family of Calcutta, thundered at a Doubting Thomas who admitted that he had regarded the Master as a god but could not regard Mother as a goddess: "Do you then believe that God married the daughter of a mere hewer of cow dung cakes [*ghuntekudunir meye*]?[69] It may be that calling the young widow a goddess was the most respectable way of allaying her misgivings, as well as society's, about her association with young monks.

IX

Sarada's status as the Holy Mother was publicized internationally by Vivekananda, who was also responsible for the universally revered image of Ramakrishna as a Vedantin. Most probably, the swami admired Sarada's selfless devotion to her husband and felt sorry for her austere life,[70] and was grateful for her particular generosity to him. In a lecture at Pasadena, California, he spoke of the utterly helpless situation he and his monastic brethren had found themselves in after the demise of the Master. This misery increased manifold when his family life, following his father's sudden death, was utterly disrupted. "Oh, the agony of those days! I was living in hell," the swami confessed. "Who would sympathise with me? None— except one. That one's sympathy brought blessing and hope. She was a woman."[71] This woman was his guru's wife, Saradamani the Holy Mother. He confessed to his "fanaticism" in respect of the Holy Mother to his *gurubhai* (monastic brother) Swami Shivananda (Taraknath Ghosal) and declared: "Of Ramakrishna, you may claim, my brother, that he was an incarnation or whatever else you may like, but shame on those who have no devotion for Ma." The swami even called her *jyanta Durga* (real-life Durga) and resorted to his characteristic hyperbole so as to exalt Sarada's status above that of his guru, Ramakrishna: "Let Ramakrishna disappear, that does not frighten me. But it will be a calamity if people forget Mother. . . . Her grace on me is one hundred thousand times greater than that of the Master. . . . Brother, when I think of Mother, I say to myself: 'Who the hell is this Ramakrishna (*koh Ramah* [Ramakrishna])?'"[72]

He also became aware of the efficacy of female power and leadership in the United States, where, on his own admission, he saw how much India lagged behind the Western world in recognizing the worth of women. He not only found the American women "very beautiful" but also possessed of divine attributes.[73] He apparently was shrewd enough to realize the potential for a mother figure in his projected Vedanta movement in the absence of a charismatic male guru figure. Thus the wife of his late guru needed to be elevated to a divine status in order to project her as the living embodiment of the Ramakrishna ideal he was preaching in the West. He therefore declared that "Mother is the incarnation of Bagala in the guise of Saraswati."[74] He agreed with Yogananda's remark made as early as 23 April 23 1890, that if Ramakrishna was Ishwara (God), "she must be the *Ishwari*."[75] Vivekananda also wished to publicize the image of the Holy Mother as the living exemplar of ideal Indian womanhood, as the embodiment of divinity—*jyanta Durga*—and finally as the inspiration behind his projected Ramakrishna movement in India and overseas. "Mother has come to re-awaken *mahashakti* in India, and following her the Gargis and Maitreyis will be reborn in this world. That is why we must build a *math* for Mother," the swami pleaded in his letter to Shivananda.[76]

Vivekananda had a similar agenda for publicizing his guru Ramakrishna's status. He had told his acquaintance Prasannakumar Shastri in 1899 that he never gave a sermon on the Master's avatarhood.[77] He was deeply disappointed with SriM's English version of the diary *Kathamrita* that had transformed Ramakrishna into a sectarian divinity. He wrote to his *gurubhai* (brother monk) Swami Trigunatitananda (Saradaprasanna Mitra) from overseas that statements like "Ramakrishna Paramahamsa is God" would not fly in the West.[78] Swamiji had earlier advised his other *gurubhai,* Swami Ramakrishnananda (Shashibhusan Chakravarti), to keep in mind the fact that the entire world was listening to "our every word and watching our every move" and therefore to be cautious and circumspect in what he said and wrote.[79] Clearly, for Swami Vivekananda, Ramakrishna as a male spiritual leader had to be presented in a rational and sensible manner, whereas his wife's status as a goddess was not so outlandish, as most Bengalis were used to regarding their mother in divine terms—something acceptable as a mark of respect and not to be bothered about so much. Sarada as a living goddess was one thing, but the *paramahamsa* as a world-class leader had to be of the real world, and the swami publicized his guru as a Vedantic superman.[80] Thus, the assertion of Saradamani's divinity was more an indication of affection—a gift of her husband's influential disciples—than a really serious and well-thought-out attempt at apotheosis. However, as we shall see later, Sarada did succeed in earning a reputation as a goddess from her Bengali devotees and admirers. She came to impersonate either Kali, Bagala, or Annapurna—various forms of the Mother Goddess of folklore and tradition.

Swami Vivekananda (1863–1902)

5

Saradamani's Divine Motherhood

No doubt, the songs of the eighteenth-century *sadhaka* ascetics like
Ramprasad and Kamalakanta described the Primal Energy, Adyashakti,
but She was the goddess of the imagination and could never be transformed into a worldly mother. The birth of Sri Ramakrishna's wife filled
a void not only in the history of India but in the annals of the world as
well.

—Pravrajika Vedantaprana, "Lokajanani"

I

VIVEKANANDA'S PERSONAL AGENDA FOR PROCLAIMING SARADAMANI'S DIVINE
motherhood was facilitated by her ability to act out the role of an ideal
Indian mother and to assume the iconographical posture of the Hindu goddess. She not only insisted that she *was* the goddess Bhagavati or Jagajjanani
(Mother of the Universe)[1] and even put up with severe physical pain inflicted by eager devotees anxious to be remembered by their Holy Mother,
but she also unhesitatingly (though unconceitedly) playacted the role of a
living divine. Once she wore a white sari, and with the locks of her hair
falling on the back and with a grave but serene countenance, she assumed
the pose of a fear-dispelling divinity by raising her right hand *(abhayamudra)*
and bade a young devotee, Nareshchandra, to bring white and yellow flowers.
Awestruck, Naresh promptly procured the flowers and with hands trem-
bling in ecstatic excitement began to offer them to her feet. She then or-
dered him to adorn her right foot with white flowers (reportedly Ramakrishna
used to prefer white flowers) and the left foot with yellow. The reporter of
this scene writes: "Is this a manifestation of her Bagala identity? It seems
Mother is the representation of all goddesses [*sarvadeviswarupini*]."[2]

Ashutosh Mitra describes the "unprecedented and unimaginable spectacle" of Sarada's worship as a living Durga with flower and sandal paste

71

along with the ritual worship of the Durga image during Durgapuja festival around 1903.[3] On another occasion, at Kothar in Orissa (family estates of Balaram Basu), she calmly allowed Surendranath Sarkar and two fellow devotees to worship her feet with flowers. She even arranged to have the flowers brought for the purpose and accepted the oblations standing. When her young devotees confessed to their innocence of Sanskrit mantras for the ritual, she advised them to offer flowers only, cautioning them to avoid offering the *dhutura* (Datura) flower, as it was meant for Shiva worship only.[4] Similarly, she instructed her devotee Sarayu Ray, who considered the Holy Mother as Jagajjanani, on how to worship her with flowers.[5]

The continuum of divinity and maternity in Saradamani's public image is fittingly expressed in Ashutosh Sengupta's description of the Holy Mother sitting on her bed as an imperial goddess *(rajarajeshwari)* with her two feet on the ground, assuming the iconic form of the bliss-bestowing goddess *(barada murti)*. Sengupta was so moved by this image that he prostrated himself, mentally praying to her to help him formulate his question for her. On another occasion, he saw the Holy Mother sitting on the bed with her feet spread out and rocking an infant lovingly and gently. She was ailing at the time, but when he looked at her he saw no trace of illness on her "blessed face" and confessed to his utter inability to describe the "wonderful expression of her eyes and the supramundane beauty of that visage."[6]

Sengupta's theophanic but quasi-realistic description of the Holy Mother—intensely human and at the same time enchantingly divine—may be complemented by another description of her by a monk-devotee, Swami Saradeshananda, who saw her clad, like the goddess Lakshmi, in a white sari with thin red border. Her face partially veiled and her curly hair falling over the right breast, she was seated on the porch of her village neighbor Satish Biswas.[7] Surendranath Sen had a vision of Sarada as the goddess Saraswati in his dream. In 1906, at Kamarpukur, his head began to reel and he fell into a coma during his initiation by the Holy Mother, because Sen found an uncanny resemblance between her and the goddess of his dream.[8] In a parallel case, Nishikanta Majumdar dreamed that Mother Kali of Kalighat (Calcutta) was lifting him, like a child, with her four hands. A month later, when he saw Sarada at Jairambati carrying a vegetable and fish cutter *(banti)* in her hand, he felt the goddess of his dream had materialized in real life. Sarada was so amused and pleased with the boy's reaction that she gently massaged his body from head to knee, including his chest and back, saying, "You're a pure, enlightened, and liberated soul."[9] A certain orphaned boy, whose mother's name was Sarada, came across the Holy Mother's name while reading Akshaykumar Sen's *Ramakrishnapunthi*. He hastened to the ailing Sarada's home in Calcutta. On seeing the Holy

Mother lying in bed he had a vision, in turn, of Radha, Krishna, Ramakrishna, and Kali. He was so overwhelmed by the Kali vision that Sarada had to calm him down by touching him with her blessed hand.[10]

One of Sarada's female disciples, Kusumkumari Devi, had a vision during her initiation that Saradamani was seated naked inside a halo, giving birth to wormlike tiny human beings and eating them immediately. On being told about the vision, the Holy Mother explained that the Master made Kusum see Prikriti, that is, the Great Goddess in her creative aspect.[11] Nagendranath Chakravarti saw in Sarada with her long locks of hair a brilliantly fair woman with a large third eye in between the eyebrows.[12] Keshabchandra Nag was cured of a serious disease when he was administered, in dream, a white pill (something like a naphthalene ball) by the Holy Mother. Reportedly, his recovery astounded even his physicians.[13] Swami Shivananda (Mahapurus Maharaj) is quoted as telling his disciple Swami Nirvanananda after Sarada's death that the ground of the Belur Math was superior to the fifty-one *pithas* (holy shrines), because the former could boast of the remains of the entire body of the goddess Sati whereas each of the latter contained only a limb of the goddess.[14]

II

Saradamani's divine reputation among her devotees and disciples speaks volumes of their bhakti. It is they who delighted in seeing a goddess in someone whom they genuinely loved and adored. In fact, one of her disciples from eastern Bengal, Surendranath Bandyopadhyay, asserted categorically that Sarada was truly a mother to him and never a goddess such as Vishwajanani or Jagajjanani.[15] Even Sarada herself was aware of her identity as a human mother. "I am your true mother," she once reminded Girish Ghosh, "a mother not by virtue of being your Guru's wife, nor because of any assumed relationship, nor by way of empty talk, but your own true mother."[16] When Ashutosh Mitra, delirious with high fever, clasped her feet and insisted on knowing her true identity, she told him calmly and firmly that he need not trouble himself in that regard, because she was his mother. When Ashu calmed down and inquired if he could count on her affection for all time, she reassured him with a thundering "yes."[17]

Saradamani's Holy Mother figure and her divine identity were also an apotheosis of the motherly qualities adored in Bengali culture. Bengalis idealize their mother above everybody and everything. A typical Bengali rhetorical outburst for a mother figure is revealed in a letter to Sarada from an eager devotee of the late *paramahamsa*. The devotee described himself as her "crazy son" and "mad son, Manomohan," confessing that he had talked a lot in his "emotional fervor."[18] Sushilkumar Sarkar became crazy with ecstatic delight when he worshiped the Holy Mother's feet with flowers and left her "as if intoxicated." When she spoke to him for the first time, he was stunned in a kind of hypnotic spell *(mantramugdhabat haiya)* and wept. Seeing his condition, Sarada passed her hand over his head. He placed his head at her feet, and thereupon his mind "took a trip to the realm of ecstasy [*bhavarajya*]."[19] The supersentimental and divinely crazy Durgacharan Nag could only totter near the staircase of the Holy Mother's house. He was in no condition to climb the stairs and had to be carried upstairs. Even a senior monk like the highly respected Brahmananda used to tremble in emotion whenever he met her.[20]

Another instance of a typical devotional exuberance comes from the childlike behavior of a *brahmachari* (monastic initiate) named Yadu, a young man from eastern Bengal with a Bengali accent, the so-called *bangal bhasa*, which Calcutta's *bhadralok babus* used to make fun of. Sometime in June 1911 he visited Jairambati along with Saradananda and others. It was a rainy evening accompanied with thunderstorm. Just to tease the bucolic *bangal* boy, Saradananada advised "Yodo" (a familiar slang term for "Yadu") to pick 108 lotuses and offer them at the Holy Mother's feet, assuring him of unlimited merits *(punya)* and provoking him to show off the degree of his devotion and enterprise to the monks. The swami was actually kidding the young man, but Yadu swallowed the bait and rushed out of the home in search of the sacred flowers. Since it was pitch-dark outside, the intrepid *bangal* found his way to the field in the illumination from the lightning and collected the material for the ritual worship. When he finally returned and offered the lotuses at Sarada's feet, the Holy Mother did not utter a word but calmly placed her hand in a gesture of blessing the devotee. Saradananda, of course, worried over the possibility that the crazy daredevil might have caught cold.[21]

III

Strangely enough, for the Hindus, and especially Bengalis, the idealized mother is detached from female sexuality. A mother is an immaculate female figure for both monks and householders. Swami Vivekananda declared in his lecture "Women of India": "Is woman a name to be coupled with the physical body only? . . . No, no! Woman! Thou shalt not be coupled with anything connected with flesh. The name has been called holy once and for ever, for what name is there which no lust can ever approach, no

carnality even come near, than the one word mother?" The monk's senti-
ment was fully shared by his elder cousin, the householder *gurubhai*
Ramchandra Datta, who wrote of Saradamani's holy motherhood in his
Jibanbrittanta: "After all she was no ordinary wife. Could the wife of someone who was the master of thousands of [spiritual] orphans . . . deign to
acquire the habits of beasts given to sexual appetites? The scriptures ap-
prove of [the union of] man and woman for begetting a son. O Ma, you are
mother to thousands of sons and daughters. Do you have to lower yourself
to the status of dogs and jackals?"[22]

The same woman who is lambasted in Hindu scripture and culture as a
sexual being is elevated to divinity as an immaculate mother. In other words,
Hindu culture apotheosizes motherhood by making it an idealized abstrac-
tion. A woman becomes a holy mother, but she is denied biological and
natural motherhood. Sarada's personal tragedy as a wife deprived of a natural
and legitimate love life was transformed into her apotheosis as an immaculate mother. It is as a mother that Sarada was deified, and her most popular
divine identity was that of the benevolent goddess Jagajjanani, one of the
numerous appellations of the goddess Kali. Yet she was never seen as the
traditional Kali by her mainline devotees, that is, those who were the disciples and devotees of the late *paramahamsa* and those who were mature
adults from the workaday world. They regarded her as Mother or Universal
Mother at all times. As far as can be determined from contemporary sources
and modern studies, there were only a handful of individuals who wished
to see or actually did see her as Kali: Swami Premananda (Baburam Ghosh),
the child Shivaram (Shibu), an anonymous orphaned boy, the youthful
Nishikanta, a devotee named Surendranath Sen, the drunkard Padmavinod,
and more recently, a scholar-monk of the Ramakrishna Order, Swami
Abjajananda.[23]

Swami Premananda sincerely believed that Sarada *was* actually the
goddess Kali of Kalighat (Calcutta). He advised Swami Nirvanananda to
go to Udbodhana (Sarada's Calcutta home) before visiting the Kali temple
at Kalighat. When Nirvanananda related his conversation with Premananda
to Sarada, she smiled a little, adding: "Baburam is right, my son."[24] The
man who always regarded her as Kali in her traditional image of the Terrible Mother was Padmabinod (Binodbihari Som), a stage actor at Girish
Ghosh's theater and an incorrigible drunkard, who managed to have his last
booze in sickbed dying of dropsy. This idiosyncratic and intrepid devotee,
father of a teenage son, habitually visited Sarada's residence at night after
consuming his daily quota of *karanabari* (alcoholic beverage, in the tantric
lexicon) and sang to her from across the street. He once serenaded her with
the words,

Because you like *shmashan* [cremation grounds]
   I made my heart a *shmashan*
For you, O Shyama, the dweller of the *shmashan*,
So that you'll keep dancing [here] all the time.
I've strewn ashes all around waiting for you.
Hurl Mahakal [Shiva], conqueror of death, at your feet.
Come dancing to me, O Ma,
And I shall behold your vision with my eyes closed.[25]

Som would leave only after she reciprocated his solicitations by lifting up the blinds of her room. Even though her sleep was thus interrupted, Sarada told her disciple Durgapuri that she did not mind the disturbance at all, as she could not help but respond to his piteous call.[26] Most others saw in Saradamani the image of a benign and bountiful deity, and even those who beheld Kali in her (with the sole exception of the wayward Padmabinod) saw the goddess not in her typical terrible form but as a magnanimous and magnificent mother figure. She also appears to have indulged in Padmabinod's overflowing devotion for her, knowing perfectly well that Som was quite conscious of his exuberance. She confided to her devotees that he behaved that way even with all his senses intact *(jnan tantane)*.[27]

According to Abjajananda, the Holy Mother deliberately concealed her *swarupa* (real identity). Even her wearing a veil *(ghomta),* a common enough practice with married women or widows in Bengal, has been interpreted as her *yogamaya*, illusion, her mysterious cover *(rahasyamayi avaran)*. The swami finds a strong confirmation of his belief in her divine identity in the conversation of a visitor. This man, referred to as a distinguished monastic son of the Holy Mother *(srisrimar janaika vishista-santan),* once told Sarada that she must be the Mother of the Universe, because she had herself admitted that her husband was Brahman himself—*Purnabrahman Sanatana.*[28] Swami Satswarupananda could not realize that Mother was divine when he first met her in 1919. Her stature and her countenance reminded him of his own grandmother. Later the swami reflected on the reasons for his inability to detect her divinity. He came to realize that Mother had hidden her *swarupa* behind her maya, which also blocked his vision and stunned his intelligence. "Perhaps I was not ready then," the swami reflected.[29] Devotees besides Abjajananda sincerely believed that the Holy Mother deliberately concealed her real identity. When one of them, Swami Ishanananda, asked her why she did not remember her *swarupa*, she replied with characteristic candor and conviction: "My son, how could I remember my real identity all the time? How else could I carry on my duties? But know what? If I wish, I can experience sudden illumination at the slightest thought even when I am busy, and can understand the play of *mahamaya* [Great Illusion]."[30]

V

Gradually Saradamani became an adept at assuming the divine role popular in the folk mind. She is reported to have behaved like the goddess Bagala and overpowered her late husband's disciple Harish Mustafi, who had turned insane temporarily and chased her at Kamarpukur. As she recalled, Sarada controlled the mad Mustafi by pulling his tongue out and subduing him physically.[31] At times she would impersonate the terrible Kali of folklore and scripture *(bhim bhavani karali)*. When a devotee jestingly wondered what would happen if the temple of the goddess at Kamarpukur (meaning Sarada's home after marriage) were gutted by fire, she yelled "Fine—fine! That would then be a cremation ground just as the Master would have preferred." She then burst into a peal of laughter *(attahasi):* "Hah, hah, hah!" The unsuspecting devotee, of course, missed the humor and stared at her dumbstruck, as if he saw the goddess herself.[32] However, she was also sensible enough to be aware of the extent to which such impersonations could go. When the young Ashutosh Mitra insisted on being told in plain terms that she had willed her Kali *swarupa* to be manifest to the low-caste robber couple on the field of Telobhelo (near Arambagh in Bankura), she told him that it was the robber himself who saw the goddess in her. However, Ashutosh begged her not to assume divine personality for him but remain his mother. Sarada was amused as well as pleased to be relieved of the onerous Kali posture, which called for standing up and sticking the tongue out.[33] When Nivedita entreated her to assume Kali's persona, Saradamani replied jestingly: "No, my dear, I can't be Kali. I would have to stick my tongue out all the time."[34]

One day while sweeping her room she felt tired and murmured to herself: "I can't do it any more. I can't finish the job even with my unlimited [*ananta*] hand." Having uttered this she stopped suddenly and with a smile told young Ritananda sitting nearby: "Look, I've just a pair of hands and yet I'm saying to myself that I've unlimited hands, what's this!"[35] When Swami Keshavananda (Taraknath Datta), head of Koalpara Ashrama, told Sarada that after her "no one will revere goddesses like Shashthi and Shitala," she protested: "Why not? They are my parts."[36] She in fact claimed calmly: "I am Bhagavati [Goddess], the Divine Mother of the Universe."[37] On another occasion, she confidently told a devotee who remarked that people regarded her as a goddess: "Why should people have to say all this? I am saying it."[38] Chandramohan Datta of Vikrampur (Dhaka) reports how the Holy Mother obliged his craving for an epiphany by transforming herself into the goddess Jagaddhatri in a blaze of light. Before assuming the visage of the deity, Sarada had cautioned Chandramohan that no one but he would be able to behold that image, adding that he must not be afraid when he beheld her real identity and that he should never tell anyone of this experience as long as she lived.[39] She similarly appeared as the bountiful and beautiful and resplendent goddess Jagaddhatri to a young girl named Basanabala Nandy, who beheld the vision after having been awakened suddenly from her sleep.[40]

VI

Though Sarada believed herself to be really a goddess in human form, she nevertheless was almost casual and never arrogant. Swami Prabhavananda recalls that the Twice-blessed Holy Mother always stayed calm and indifferent to the worships she received from her innumerable devotees.[41] One reason for her remarkable humility as a *deus homo* might be the fact that her divine identity was derived primarily from her relationship with the *paramahamsa* the God-man. She told a devotee that the Master was truly God in human form who moved about in disguise and left the world once his identity was revealed.[42] When a devotee asked Sarada if she, as the wife of the Master, who was a Purnabrahman (Brahman in Its fullness), was aware of her own status, she told her that she was actually the goddess Lakshmi, whose proper place is by the side of her husband, Narayana, in Baikuntha, and that she had assumed a human body because of maya.[43] Similarly, she defended her involvement in the quotidian hassles of her family life—which were queried by a woman at Baranasi—by saying that her entrapment in mundane problems was caused by her maya.[44]

Sarada was often tormented and verbally abused by a crazy aunt of hers. She would try to prevent her from further outbursts by pleading to her not to harass her any more. Otherwise, her real self that was hidden inside her human body would be provoked, and no one, not even the trinity of Brahma, Vishnu, and Maheswara, would be able to control her. She cautioned her tormentor against taking her for granted as a harmless creature, and said that no one in the whole world could save her if she, Sarada, wanted to punish her.[45] This was an unmistakable echo of her husband's warning to his unmannerly nephew Hriday, who once subjected Sarada to severe verbal abuse.[46]

Sometimes Sarada had to pay a price for her exalted status. Once a young man visited Udbodhana with a view to worshiping her with flowers. On seeing the stranger she covered herself with a heavy sheet and sat on the bed with her feet dangling, to which the visitor offered flowers and his *pranam* (salutation). He then sat down on the floor "like a log of wood" to practice yoga. Meanwhile Sarada was perspiring profusely. When her factotum Golap-ma (Golapsundari Devi) came to the room and saw the devotee sitting in the same posture as Sarada, she pulled him up and admonished him: "Have you taken her for a lifeless wooden deity whom you wish to bring to life by your yoga? Don't you have any sense? Mother has become restless due to sweating!"[47] Gambhirananda describes Sarada's predicament of being deified by her devotees, who even inflicted acute physical pain on her by literally biting or otherwise hurting her limbs in order to be remembered by the Holy Mother.[48]

She, however, endured such persecutions of adoration with perfect equanimity.[49] When a devotee suggested that people should not touch Mother's feet because it caused her suffering, she reassured him that she felt no pain if a genuine devotee touched her feet. She added that she had come to the world to accept people's sins and sorrows. She, however, acknowledged that she felt pain when degenerate people touched her feet, but she permitted her devotee to salute her by touching her feet.[50] On another occasion, a famous pandit saluted Mother by placing his head on her feet; and grasping both her legs, he began to sob loudly, beseeching her to awaken his consciousness (chaitanya) by placing her feet on his head. As was her practice with adult male strangers, Sarada sat covered from head to toe with a thick sheet made in Bombay (bombai chadar) and perspired heavily, but the intrepid pandit would not budge. His escort, Ramchandra Majumdar, angrily pointed out that he was tormenting her and told him to release Sarada's feet, assuring him that his desires would surely be fulfilled, as he had seen and saluted the Holy Mother. She likewise reassured the prostrate devotee that he would succeed in realizing his desires.[51]

Such emotional outbursts constituted the daily fare of the Holy Mother's public life. As Satyendranath Majumdar writes:

> There was no end to the merciful Mother's sufferings. . . . She was endowed with the qualities of forbearance and forgiveness. Some afternoons I used to be in charge of lining up the devotees before bringing them to her. Some of them were real troublemakers. Middle-aged men sobbed loudly [bheu bheu kare kandchhe], their heads [on the ground]. Some went on relating their woes and worries oblivious of others waiting in line. Some remained totally still, having placed their head on her feet. One day one of them just lay on his back and began to entreat her to place her feet on his chest to impart [divine] consciousness.

Majumdar found such lachrymose lunacy utterly silly and once made fun of these characters before Mother. She told him: "When you grow up you'll understand the sufferings of unfortunate people. The fact is you're not a mother."[52]

VIII

Saradamani, then, remained throughout her life a quintessential mother of the household possessed of affectionate disposition and quiet authority. The mother–Holy Mother fusion leading to her apotheosis owed significantly to her devotees and admirers, who either saw in her the image of a demure Jagajjanani or a dashing Jagaddhatri or the terrible Kali, though the Holy Mother by her character and conduct contributed immeasurably to the humanization of the goddess whom Rachel McDermott has described as the "One with the Lolling Tongue."[53] Though some feminist scholars in India and in the West see Kali as the subverter of patriarchal values, it was her image as a mother that proved to be popular and enduring.[54] Swami Purnatmananda has provided wonderful anecdotes from three different countries—India, Bangladesh, and the United States—showing how an unlettered rickshaw-puller of Calcutta, a simple tea vendor on the road from Dhaka to Jessore, and an educated woman of Hollywood all found in Sarada's photograph a compelling reminder of their own mothers.[55] Let Sarada's "devotee-children" have the final say on her humanity and divinity:

> [T]he Holy Mother stands out as a unique example, whose utter innocence could melt even the hardest of hearts, who never looked at the faults of others, whose love never made any distinction between the deserving and the undeserving, in whose eyes the saint and the sinner were alike her precious children, whose heart held all humanity in its maternal embrace, and who considered it a privilege to labour and to suffer for even the least of them. If we cannot see here the face of the all-loving Universal Mother, of God the Redeemer, where else can we?[56]

It must be noted that Saradamani's devotees actually saw in her not just the resemblance of their human mothers but an incarnation of the abstracted and idealized Mother Goddess. That is why Swami Vivekananda, who was a master of high-blown rhetoric and hyperbole, once proclaimed that the Holy Mother was his "only mother."[57] Thus Sarada's mother-Holy Mother identity is actually a theological expression of an idealized cultural construct. Sarada performed the three roles–the role of a earthly mother in looking after the material comforts of her "children," that of a Holy Mother in being their spiritual guide as the bestower of *diksha*, and that of Mother of the Universe (Jagajjanani) by assuming the iconographic posture of the Great Goddess in her various aspects: Jagaddhatri, Kali, Annapurna, and Durga, respectively. As a successful performer of these familiar feminine functions, she was packaged as a cultural icon by her clients in the spiritual marketplace of Hindu Bengal.

In the final analysis, Saradamani's blending of mother and Holy Mother exemplifies the unique *unio mystica* of Vaishnava spirituality that is the hallmark of Bengali devotional culture. Sarada endeared herself to her myriads of devotees, disciples, and visitors not only as a grace-giving goddess but as a food-providing compassionate mother. Her apotheosis through her sacred maternity makes sense when we are reminded of the quintessential Hindu spiritual alchemy whereby the distant and transcendental deity of the high heavens dissolves into our near and dear ones: *debatare priya kari, priyere debata* (we cherish our gods as our own and transform our loved ones into a divinity). What Bengal's greatest poet, the Nobel Laureate Rabindranath Tagore, wrote in the true spirit of a son of the soil could very well match the idealized image of his unlettered contemporary, the Holy Mother, by her devotees and disciples:

> I know now God offers affection in the form
> of a mother,
> in the form of a son He accepts it again.
> In the form of a donor He gives,
> > he takes again in the form of the poor.
> > As a disciple He shows his devotion,
> As a teacher He gives his blessings.
> As a beloved breaking the stony heart
> he raises it in the fountain of love.
> He is all attached; he is also the renouncer.
> In this God's teeming universe,
> I have cast the net of my heart:
> the entire world is drawing me, pulling
> into the lap of its love.[58]

6

Saradamani's Maternal Triumph

Considering she lived in an age when male chauvinism was at its greatest height—when women in our society were at the complete mercy of
the male members of their families—Sarada Devi projected a highly
independent mind.

—Shreela Roy, "Sarada Devi:
Relevance for the Modern Indian Woman"

I

SARADA PREFERRED TO BE A REAL-LIFE MOTHER TO HER SURROGATE CHILDREN.
Most probably this preference acted as a compensation for her unrequited
maternal desires. Saradamani's parents, especially her mother, Shayama-
sundari, often regretted her daughter's marriage to a crazy young man and
is reported to have lamented: "What a pity that we wed our Sarada to a
madcap! She neither has a home nor children and did not get to hear the
call of mother." Once Ramakrishna overheard his mother-in-law's regrets
and told her: "Mother, have no regrets over this. Your daughter will eventually come to have so many children that she will have no peace of mind due
to their crying 'Mother' all the time." He even once asked his wife bluntly:
"Do you harbor a desire to have children?" Sarada responded: "No, I do
not want anything except your happiness." He then assured her: "All right,
you will have many good sons."[1] He made a solemn promise to his wife at
Dakshineshwar that he would leave her children unavailable even to those
who perform the severest austerities. He even entreated his devotees such
as Ram Datta and a few others to visit with Sarada at the *nahabat:* "Look,
[she] is bugging me for a son. Please go to the *nahabat* and tell her that you
are really her sons."[2]

After his death, when she despaired alone at Kamarpukur that she had
neither a son nor anything else and wondered about her future, she had a

vision of the Master and heard him say to her that he had left her many jewels of sons even though she had wanted only one and that she would have many more in time.[3] Whether Sarada did actually see her dead husband or hear him speak to her, Ramakrishna's promise and prophecy proved remarkably accurate. Within a short time after his death Sarada's thwarted human motherhood was sublimated into a compensatory divine motherhood. In other words, Saradamani became not just a *ma*—that is, a mother—but Srima, the Blessed Mother or Holy Mother, a mother by divine right. She not only became a goddess but by the same token a mother to her husband's devotees, followers, and admirers, who enjoyed her sumptuous hospitality and her affectionate attention to their physical and emotional comfort; and they proclaimed her divine motherhood proudly and loudly.

She remained throughout her life a loving, nurturing, and compassionate maternal figure—never a matriarch—of the Ramakrishna Order. She truly was, as Vivekananda said, *sanghajanani*—"mother of the Order."[4] Brahmachari Akshaychaitanya has documented comments and observations from Saradamani's numerous devotees on her motherly care and affection for all her guests and visitors. He has written about the manifestations of her motherhood: she prayed for the material as well as spiritual welfare for her children and cooked food for them untiringly. She would not only oblige their most outlandish demands without demur but also suffer pain by accepting secretly the sins and sicknesses of her visitors. Additionally, as their spiritual mentor, she helped them achieve true knowledge and salvation.[5]

The *brahmachari*'s observation could be substantiated by several instances of Mother's hospitality. Swami Virajananda (Kalikrishna Basu) recalls his first meeting with the Holy Mother:

> How happy she was with us! She could not decide where to put us up, what to cook for us! She toiled day and night for all this. She got busy cooking a variety of dishes for the two [major] meals of the day and watched us eat and forced us to take second helpings. We have never tasted such nectarean meals. . . . Because our [late] Master used to enjoy lentils and poppy seed curry and a fish preparation [*maach chatui*] and because Mother used to coax us to eat, we used to gorge ourselves with double the amount for a single man. That cooking was too delicious to describe. It was as if "ethereal something." I can still savor its taste.

About his spiritual experience or enlightenment Virajananda writes: "We had nothing to do but meditate occasionally, gossip, stuff ourselves, sleep, or go for a walk along the banks of the Amodar River."[6] Spiritual gain, if any, consisted in personal feelings of profound satisfaction. To quote the swami once more:

Mother never allowed us to stay for more than one night at Kamarpukur, the Master's birthplace, because she felt that we would face problems of food and stuff. While staying there we used to be filled with a powerful holiness, happiness, and well-being and felt that "we are treading on holy ground . . . vibrant with spirituality." It seemed as if this place was out of this world![7]

Swami Prabhavananda recalls how the Twice-blessed Holy Mother resembled his own birth mother, who was a simple, easygoing rustic woman. Sarada's unique quality was that she resembled the mothers of her intimate devotees.[8] Sarada had an instinctive understanding of what her devotees needed. Labanyakumar Chakravarti writes that after he had been ministered the *diksha* by Mother, she had not placed her hand on his head. However, Sarada did realize her oversight and sent for the young initiate to come back to her for the missed blessing.[9]

II

Swami Bodhananda (Haripada Chattopadhyay) writes about foods and feasts at Jairambati where the Holy Mother, assisted by cooks and helpers, used to be busy preparing meals for the visitors till eleven at night.[10] Swami Bishuddhananda (Jitendranath Datta) was treated with a glass of milk at night when the young man first visited Mother and wrote: "Mother was a perfect image of humility, modesty, simplicity, and purity. Though she possessed the highest spiritual knowledge and experience, she was above all mother. This is her best identity."[11] Nilkanta Chakravarti had a pleasant and sumptuous meal of meat and fish at Jairambati and saw Sarada bidding him good-bye with tearful eyes. He wrote: "The idea came naturally to my mind—she is my mother of many births, my eternal mother, truly my mother."[12]

Indeed, Sarada's hospitality was phenomenal. Swami Saradeshananda provides a graphic description of her involvement with food and cooking:

I am amazed to think of Ma's astonishingly keen eyes for [details]. Whenever devotees from different regions gathered at Jairambati, she would advise the cook auntie [*randhuni masi*] on exactly how much and what each of them would like to eat, including even the number of unleavened bread pieces [*ruti*]. That is why her children were so satisfied with their meal at Mother's. To quote the Master: "Ma knows exactly who among her children could digest what!"

The swami adds that she would eat with her female devotees only after all the men were fed and would eat upon the return of anyone among the men who had gone out without his meal.[13] Almost all her devotees being Bengali, who are fish lovers, she would arrange for fish preparations at her Calcutta abode, Udbodhana, every day. Then she would distribute betel leaf preparation—that is *pan*—after the meal and would be very happy to see the boys chew the mouth refresher.[14] On his first visit to Jairambati Swami Abhayananda recalls how he was utterly scandalized to see the Holy Mother sitting on the ground baking *ruti* for her visitors from Calcutta. He was similarly shocked to find her going in the early hours of the morning to fetch fresh milk for the morning tea of her urban guests.[15]

One of her visitors confessed with disarming candor that he didn't go to Srima for religious instructions, nor did he care if she was superior to ordinary women. On the way to his in-laws' home he used to take a short rest at Mother's home at Jairambati, and she used to offer him puffed rice, molasses, and water for refreshment. Enjoying this simple fare at her place became his habit, and he could never feel satisfied without them.[16] Another young devotee, Gokul, once sang along with his friend Manmathanath Chattopadhyay of Tajpur village (husband of Ramakrishna's mentally deranged niece Radhu) behind closed doors at Kamarpukur:

> I won't go to my mother again.
> I won't ask for food again
> Even when hungry.

Then he beheld Saradamani taking on the persona of the supreme goddess *(rajarajeshwari)*. With a radiant countenance, she carried two plates of snacks in both hands, opened the door, and placed them on the ground, saying, "Eat now." As Gokul recalls, her behavior and visage that afternoon were so tremendous and touching *(sundar o marmasparsi)* that he remembered the spectacle all his life.[17] Nirvanananda recalls his meeting with the Holy Mother in 1914 and how she insisted on nourishing and nursing him to health (he looked pale and thin) before he could leave for Uttarakhand for his austerities *(tapasya)*.[18] "Never torment your body," Saradamani advised a female visitor named Mrinalini. "You must eat something. Too much fasting is not good. How would you perform your spiritual duties if your body fails?"[19] Sarada's generosity and relentless striving to keep her visitors, disciples, and devotees satisfied and comfortable brought her the reputation of a renunciant of sorts—that of a selfless and tireless mother to all her children.

III

Sarada's principal concern for food preparation and distribution, which made her appear as the grace-and-grub-bestowing goddess Annapurna (literally, "stuffed with foods"), was in fact an eloquent testimony to her femininity, even in a cross-cultural perspective. A mother's passion, writes Elias Canetti, "is to give food."[20] She in fact gives her own body to be consumed by her children from conception in the womb down to the breast-feeding stage, and subsequently looks after their creature comforts till they grow to be independent adults. This maternal sacrifice transmutes itself into an unconscious (and often unintended) strategy for control and domination. Caroline Bynum observes in the context of medieval society of Europe that for women food is the easiest thing to give away in a male-dominated-and-controlled society.[21] This observation is equally valid for Hindu society even to this day. During her husband's lifetime Sarada had regularly cooked for his devotees and visitors. Here we recall her own statement how she was importuned in respect of her personal natural comforts.[22] As the Holy Mother of the Ramakrishna Order, Sarada's world was dominated by monks whose spiritual virility consisted in renouncing women and sex but who exhibited an extraordinary fondness, even sheer weakness, for food.

Instances testifying to Saradamani's motherly affection and care for her devotes and visitors such as the ones mentioned above may be multiplied manifold. All accounts of her life agree that most people visited her at Jairambati, Kamarpukur, or Udbodhana in Calcutta mainly to obtain two satisfactions—meals and mantras. Everybody found her generous with food and ever ready to impart *diksa* (initiation). Food and shelter provided material comfort. Initiation provided spiritual merits, that, in most cases, amounted to nothing more than a psychological certainty of being inoculated against sins, as it were. It is doubtful that all initiates wanted to be ascetics or mendicants, though a few—only a handful of them—did opt for a renunciant's career. Nevertheless, many such candidates for monkhood changed their mind after having been assured by Sarada that they had accumulated enough merits to forgo the tribulations of monastic austerities.[23]

Saradamani, thus, came to preside over a community that had initially been formed by her husband and his coterie of intimate *(antaranga)* disciples. In spite of the Master's connection with the goddess Kali and his proclamation of his wife's divinity, the Ramakrishna community during his lifetime and the Ramakrishna Order following his death were associations that privileged Ramakrishna over other authorities, human or divine. In fact, as we have noted earlier, one of Ramakrishna's influential lay devotees, Ram Datta, refused to acknowledge the identity of his guru's widow. However, Sarada's emergence as the central figure of the order owed significantly to a few conscientious and determined monastic disciples of the Master, the chief among who were Vivekananda, Saradananda, Yogananda, Premananda, and Niranjanananda, and his influential and powerful lay disciple, the flamboyant Girish Ghosh. Her personality and conduct led to the flourishing of a *communio sanctorum* that was more like an extended family where the sacred and the secular coexisted in merry confusion rather than a dry and dreary ascetic association of world-weary renunciants. The preeminently human character of the Holy Mother's following is a testimony to her monumental maternal triumph.

7

Sarada's Formative Years:
Travels and Tribulations of the *Sanghajanani*

> The Ramakrishna Order is like a big family. The Twice-blessed Mother
> is the mother of this family. . . . Her love nourished this order in the past
> and . . . though invisible now, she still is doing her work. . . . This is her
> obligation because she is the *sanghajanani.*
> —Lokeshwarananda, "Sanghajanani"

I

SARADA LIVED FOR THIRTY-THREE YEARS FOLLOWING HER RETURN FROM BRINDABAN
in 1887. During 1887–98 she lived a public life, keeping a low profile as a
widow except for the attention she received from the devotees and disciples of her late husband. She removed to Calcutta in the late spring of
1888, where she lodged in a rented home at Belur (near Dakshineshwar).
Golap-ma and Yogen-ma lived with her as her companions, and Swami
Trigunatitananda acted as a security guard. Sarada left for another round of
pilgrimage after a while, and this time she visited Gaya to perform the
postmortem rituals for her mother-in-law, Chandramani, as per Ramakrishna's wish. Following her return from Gaya, Sarada relocated to another home on the riverbank at Belur rented from the local landlord Nilambar
Mukherjee. Here she began receiving visitors and earning a reputation as a
holy woman, though early in November she once again traveled, this time
to Puri, site of the temple of Lord Jagannatha. She was accompanied by a
host of devotees, male as well as female, who were nicknamed *paramahamsa's* retinue *(paramahamser paltan)*. At Puri, the Srikhsetra or the
Blessed Land, Sarada had a wonderful vision that the effigy of the lord
Jagannath seemed like that of a lion among men *(purusasingha),* and she
felt like a maid attending on this God.[1]

II

On reaching Calcutta, Sarada started for Antpur, the parental village of Krishnabahabini, Balaram Basu's wife and Baburam Ghosh's (later Swami Premananda) sister. Here the influence of Balaram Basu and that of his wife, a native of Antpur, contributed a lot to Sarada's tumultuous reception. From here she made for Kamarpukur, where she stayed for a year. During this period she made occasional trips to Jairambati. She acted as hostess at her native village for a number of influential disciples of her husband, including Girish Ghosh and Niranjanananda. Even though the flamboyant and unpredictable Girish caused other devotees of Mother considerable uneasiness—this was his first encounter with Sarada—he declared Sarada the goddess of his dream when he was a teenager. He now began to proclaim the young widow's divinity and even thanked Niranjanananda for inviting him to visit Jairambati. As Girish recalled in his characteristic lingo years later: "Those *shalara* [buggers—that is, Ramakrishna's other disciples], had kept Mother hidden from us for so long. Thanks to Niranjan, I could see Mother."[2] Sarada left Jairambati for Kamarpukur and then traveled to Calcutta toward the end of 1889. This time she stayed with the family of Mahendra Gupta for a month and thereafter relocated to Balaram Basu's home. Even after Balaram's death in 1890, Sarada continued to enjoy the patronage of the Basus, who were devoted to the late *paramahamsa* and his family.

III

Later in 1890 Sarada relocated to Ghusuri. Here she reminisced about the beauty of her husband, who she said was a male with a very fair complexion (literally, of the color of *harital* or yellow orpiment) at whom the women of Kamarpukur gawked whenever he walked the village streets. Here Ramakrishna's favorite devotee, Narendranath, called on Mother, seeking her permission for his intended *pravrajya* (holy peregrination) in upper India. At Ghusuri Sarada suffered from bouts of bloody dysentery. Her condition deteriorated so much that her companion Golap-ma, who happened to be the mother-in-law of one of the scions of the influential Tagore families of the city, Sir Saurindramohan Tagore, arranged for another rented house through the latter's influence. This was the place at Barahanagar, close to Belur, where the ailing Sarada received medical treatment and recovered.

Here Sarada was visited by one of Ramakrishna' madly devoted disciples, Durgacharan Nag (Nag Mahashay), noted for his uncontrollable emotional outbursts of bhakti. His eyes were always ruddy, a condition popularly believed to have been caused by his excessive love for God *(premachakshu),* and he was thin to the point of emaciation, believed to be the result of his tremendous ascetic exercises *(kathor tapasya).* On coming to Sarada's home he experienced such a powerful emotion that his feet began to tremble and he could not walk up the stairs. When finally he managed to come up to the Holy Mother's room, he wept profusely and piteously in front of her, and was fed some sweets by her as if he were a little child. Nag departed muttering, "Ma is kinder than Father" *(baper thaikka ma dayal),* meaning Sarada was more compassionate than the Master had been.[3] Men such as the unpredictable Girish and the quite crazy Nag were the foremost and fiercest proclaimers of Sarada's divine motherhood.

IV

It is at this time, reportedly, that Sarada began manifesting a tendency to duplicate her husband's famous ecstasies. Whether these reports are part of a hagiographical strategy to proclaim Sarada's qualifications to claim her husband's spiritual/mystical heritage and continue his spiritual ministry is open to question. Nevertheless, we need to note them in order to chart her advance to the leadership position in the Ramakrishna circle. On her own admission, Sarada wished to acquire her ecstatic husband's *bhava* after she had personally witnessed his dances and trances. However, as she is reported to have said, Ramakrishna never did recommend this state for his wife. After she had told him that she never experienced *"bhab* and stuff" *(bhabtab),* Ramakrishna retorted: "What would you do with that? You will have to dance around naked [*kapad phele dhei-dhei kare nachte habey*]. Who'll take care of your clothes?"[4]

Nonetheless, Sarada succeeded in getting into ecstatic states. One rainy evening at Balaram's home, she was seen meditating and standing up and sitting down, laughing and weeping from time to time. One of her associates, Gaurdasi, hid herself under Sarada's bedstead and watched Mother's various *bhavas.* Gaurdasi spread the news of Mother's ecstasy to the members of Balaram's family. Indeed, Sarada mastered the art of her ecstatic husband's *bhava* remarkably well. Sometime in 1894, at Kalababu's grove *(kunja)* in Brindaban, she lapsed into a trancelike state while meditating. Yogen-ma repeated Lord Krishna's name in her ears for a long time, but she still was comatose. At last her bodyguard, Swami Yogananda, came and repeated Sri Ramakrishna's name, and she woke up. Yogen-ma writes that Sarada would crave food after awakened from her ecstatic state, just like the Master, who used to be ravenously hungry in his postsamadhi moments.[5] This feat of hers established two points at once: that she had become an adept at being a spiritual personality just like her husband and, more important, that her husband had in fact become superior even to God, because it was his name, not that of any canonical god, that brought her to "the physical plane."

Sarada made another holy trip to Baranasi in 1894 and revisited Gaya in the spring of 1895. At Gaya she had a wish that was to be realized later. As she confided to Yogen-ma, when she (Sarada) saw the grand assets and management of the Bodhgaya monastery, she had prayed to Ramakrishna for his blessings so that her hungry and homeless "boys," who had had to beg for food, might be able to find a shelter like this. Yogen-ma duly assured Sarada that her wishes would surely be fulfilled, as she had prayed to the Great Master.[6] Eight years later Sarada's wishes were fulfilled when the Belur Math was constructed. A hagiographical explanation of this wish fulfillment of Sarada's has been offered by citing the authority of the *Chhandogya Upanisad,* which stipulates that anyone in possession of the knowledge of Brahman could have his or her wishes fulfilled. In the same year she asked Swami Abhedananda, then departing for the West, to tell Narendranath (Swami Vivekananda), in the United States that Mother had prophesied that he would return as the conqueror of the world. Thus Sarada followed her husband in making this kind of prophecy for Narendranath. He had scribbled on his deathbed that "Naren will educate people" *(Naren lokashiksha dibe).*[7] Saradamani seemed to be progressing slowly but surely to her position of the mother of the Ramakrishna Order.

V

During 1898–1909 Sarada began her spiritual ministry. She began living in a rented home at 10/2 Bosepara Lane in the Baghbazar area of north Calcutta. Here she met the Western female disciples of Swami Vivekananda, notably Sarah Bull and Sister Nivedita. She even helped the swami, who had contracted some sort of disease after having been cursed by a Muslim fakir . Even though Sarada was honest enough to confess that she did not possess any magical powers that could cure a disease, Vivekananda relied on her hidden powers and fortuitously recovered. She was also said to be the force behind the founding of a girls' school under the leadership of Nivedita. The sister became an important channel for publicizing Mother's magnanimity and spirituality.

Sarada suffered some irreparable losses but also gained a loved one in 1899. In that year her dearest disciple, Swami Yogananda, and her dearest brother, the medical student Abhaycharan Mukhopadhyay, passed away. However, Abhay's widow, Surabala, gave birth to a girl later named Radharani or Radhu, who became the apple of Sarada's eye. Radhu turned Sarada's attention to her little family, later celebrated in her biographies as *mayer samsar* (Mother's family"). They lived at 16 Bosepara Lane, Calcutta, where Sarada began to stay in 1900. In 1902 Swami Vivekananda passed away when Sarada was at Jairambati. She returned to Calcutta on 14 February 1904 and started living at 2/1 Baghbazar Street. She developed a closer connection with Nivedita's school, located nearby. She had Swami Sarada-nanda as her caretaker at this facility. She was ailing at this time. From Nivedita's letter to Josephine MacLeod dated 24 February 1904 we come to know Sarada's physical condition: "The Holy Mother is here, so small, so thin, so dark, worn out physically, I should say, with village hardship and village life." However, the sister also stressed Sarada had the "same clear mind—same stateliness, the same womanhood, as before."[8] This year Sarada celebrated the birthday of Lord Krishna *(janmastami)* at Ramchandra Datta's retreat, Yogodyan in Kankurgachhi, and received great public acclaim.

She left for Puri in November and a few days after arrival in the holy town developed an abscess on one foot, from which she suffered for quite some time. The next two years brought further grief for her. In 1905 her uncle Nilmadhab Mukhopadhyay died, and the next year her mother, Shyamasundari, and her beloved companion and devotee Gopaler-ma passed away. In the meantime, she began receiving increasing numbers of visitors and devotees both in Calcutta and in Jairambati. In 1907 she attended the Durga Puja festival at the residence of the prominent Calcutta socialite Girish Ghosh. Following this festival Sarada's name became widely known and devotees began streaming in.

On 23 May 1909 Sarada moved into her newly built residence in Calcutta, the Udbodhana. Her spiritual ministry there lasted until her death eleven years later. In June of this year she contracted chicken pox. After her recovery she traveled to Jairambati and returned to Calcutta in January 1910. As her health still remained weak, she was advised to spend a few days at the estate of the late Balaram Basu in Kothar, and she ended up staying there for a couple of months. From Orissa Sarada proceeded to southern India to visit Rameswaram and stayed in Madras for about a month en route to Rameswaram. Here she enjoyed the hospitality of Swami Ramakrishnananda, one of the *paramahamsa*'s foremost disciples and head of the Ramakrishna monastery in Madras.

On arrival at Rameswaram in Ramnad, she was welcomed by the raja of Ramnad (who had been a devotee of Swami Vivekananda) as the "guru of my guru" and was greeted with felicitations by the royalty. Here Sarada, most probably to impress the people about her divine status, playacted an incarnation in imitation of her God-man husband. She wanted to impress upon his hosts that she had in fact been present when the image of the presiding deity of Rameswaram, Sundareshwar Shiva, and the image of Minakshi, Shiva's consort, were installed many years previously. "I see it just the same as when I placed it here," the Holy Mother quipped. When asked by a devotee what she meant, she replied with enigmatic casualness: "Never mind; I was absent-minded and it was a slip of the tongue."[9] She journeyed to Bangalore from Ramnad and finally returned to Calcutta on 11 April 1911.

After tarrying in the city for a month Sarada traveled to her natal village, Jairambati, to attend her niece Radhu's marriage. While there, she received on 1 August the shocking news of Ramakrishnananda's death. Further grief struck her later that fateful year when her beloved Irish devotee Nivedita passed away in Darjeeling on 13 October. On 5 November 1912, accompanied by the young Radhu and a number of devotees and disciples, she left for Baranasi. At Baranasi she was taken to two Ramakrishna centers—a mission (monastery) and a *sevashrama* (hospital and dispensary). Even though her ascetic husband had privileged meditation over social service, she believed that social service through this center was actually service to the Master and that this institution was touched by his presence, as it were.[10] In Baranasi Sarada was also recognized by a venerable old monk named Chameli Puri as the goddess Durga personified. Nevertheless, she elicited some adverse comments from a number of visiting women, who were shocked to see the ascetic Sarada in the midst of a family. "Mother, we see you are terribly entangled in maya," one of them complained. To this Sarada responded with characteristic calm and confirmed her own divine status: "What can I do? I myself am maya."[11] But the best and the most appropriate recognition of her demeanor as a human and humane mother came from a beggar woman whose gift of a simple fruit was accepted by Sarada graciously and gratefully. "Mother, I am a mere beggar," the raggedy donor said, weeping, "and you are so kind to me."[12]

Returning from the holy city to the metropolis, the aging and ailing Holy Mother became busy with her ministry and mentoring. She not only initiated and counseled scores of devotees and visitors but even meditated on behalf those who found no time for this practice. In the elegant prose of her monastic biographer, "[H]ers was a love that sought no tangible return nor even a word of gratitude. . . . It was a spiritual relationship that knew no barrier of time or place, caste or social position."[13]

VI

The year 1918 proved to be difficult for the old lady. She came down with an attack of malaria at the Jagadamba Ashrama, Koalpara, near her village, but she recovered following treatment by Calcutta physicians. On 30 July, she lost another of her beloved disciples, Swami Premananda. She now went back to Jairambati to continue her spiritual ministry. At the same time she also had to cope with multiple family problems. At Jairambati Sarada suffered from further bouts of malaria. However, in spite of this severe infirmity, she participated in the annual worship of Jagaddhatri according to the tradition of her family. She even divided her patrimony among her brothers and made plans for building a monastery at Jairambati. Yet there were visible signs of her gradual decline. She is reported to have told a disciple that she was feeling increasingly helpless because her duties were multiplying as her health was declining.[14] She was gradually becoming more withdrawn. She requested that her birthday, which her devotees were planning to celebrate on 13 December 1919, be observed quietly. On that day she had very high body temperature. As her condition deteriorated, Swami Saradananda, then in charge of her upkeep, suggested that she relocate to Calcutta for proper treatment.

Sarada left her natal home on 24 February 1920, this time, as it turned out, for good. She reached Udbodhana on 27 February thoroughly emaciated and with a continuous fever. Several noted Calcutta physicians—the two Ayurvedic *kabiraj* Shyamadas Bachaspati and Rajendranath Sen; the homeopath Dr. Jnanendranath Kanjilal; and the four allopaths, Drs. Bipinbihari Ghosh, Sureshchandra Bhattacharya, Nilratan Sarkar, and Prandhan Basu—tried various herbs and drugs, but to little effect. At last she was diagnosed by Dr. Basu as having contracted kala-azar, a deadly disease caused by a protozoan parasite transmitted by sand flies. The ailment affected her spleen and liver and caused her an excruciating burning sensation. When her numerous devotees and well-wishers suggested she pray to Ramakrishna for remission of pain and recovery, the levelheaded patient reminded them that her husband had suffered terribly from his terminal illness and that she could do nothing to prevent something fated to happen. While she bore her pain and suffering patiently she never ceased thinking of the physical comfort of her spiritual children. As was her wont, she remained concerned for the food and comfort of her attendants, and even of refreshments for her physicians.

On her deathbed Sarada heard about the demise of her loyal devotee Swami Adbhutananda on 24 April and of her brother Baradaprasanna on 20 May. By now she had become indifferent to feelings of attachment and grief. She might have been in intense pain and hence become somewhat numb to emotions and feelings. She began exhibiting her utter discomfiture at the sight of her dear friends and followers and relatives like Gauri-ma, Yogen-ma, and even Radhu, her dearest niece. She bluntly forbade

Gauri-ma, one of her most loyal and loving companions, to visit or touch her. She added further that if she came, she was not to enter her room but should look at her from outside the door, and warned her not to make her talk. She commanded Radhu to return to Jairambati. She even tried to get away from Radhu's child crawling toward her. "Go away, scoot. I have no attachment to any of you," the dying Sarada yelled to her niece's son. Sensing her imminent end, the compassionate human Holy Mother tried to untangle herself from all emotions and sentiments. She wanted to be free from all bondage. As she confided to Yogen-ma: "I have cut the chain of maya. No more of this."[15]

Even though Sarada the Holy Mother summoned her will to show her readiness to face death, the simple and truly loving woman in her failed to meet her end with ascetic indifference or stoic nonchalance. "Who craves for death?" she told a disciple who had asked her to exert her will to live. Toward the very end of her life Sarada was attended upon by devotees and disciples almost every hour of the day and night. She was increasingly drifting into a state of childlike helplessness. Often she would complain about being fed, as she had lost all appetite for food. She even complained of her indefatigable devotee and nurse Saralabala Sarkar (later Pravrajika Bharatiprana) that she was tormenting her by pressuring her to eat.[16] Yet the dying woman never forgot the loving attention she always received from Sarala and apologized to her for being rude.[17] For the last three days Sarada remained silent, for she had lost the power of speech. About one in the morning of Tuesday, 21 July, Sarada's end seemed imminent, and her devotees and attendants began chanting God's name. About a half hour later the Holy Mother took several deep breaths and thereupon became still. Sarada was gone. In the eyes of her devotees her face relaxed and assumed a serene mien, which they thought seemed to reflect "celestial light." Even when her corpse was consigned to fire during the cremation ceremony, one of the female devotees of the Holy Mother pointed young Sarala's gaze to the funeral pyre and exclaimed how beautifully the flames were rising up, as if to reach the heavens.[18]

Thus died a most remarkable woman who had lived a full life, even though she had been denied the normal life of a married woman. She never did experience erotic love or the filial love that a biological mother receives. Nevertheless, with her fortitude and forbearance, Saradamani transmuted her personal tragedy into a personal triumph. She became a mother to her devotees, disciples, and visitors, and they were grateful that she lived to a comparatively ripe age for her time. The Holy Mother's saga of life soon passed from history into holy remembrance. As her eloquent *sannyasini* biographer has it: "That mother, whose sight and touch made her children forget all miseries and drinking the nectar of whose words they felt the taste of supreme serenity, that Twice-blessed Mother Saradeshwari, the source of compassion and love, is no longer in the sensate world, she is now in the realm of thought and meditation."[19]

8

Sarada: An Ideal for Modern Woman?

The sacred biography of the Twice-Blessed Mother demonstrates the
path that she has shown our country. Let India be awakened to that
ideal. Let all differences among nations . . . and untouchability . . . be
wiped out forever by the examples of Mother's life. Let the disregarded
race of the mothers gain their personal rights.
—Bhumananda, *Srisrimayer Jiban-katha*

I

SARADA WAS OF COURSE MORE THAN A MERE MOTHER FIGURE. SHE WAS ALSO THE
inheritor of her late husband's spiritual leadership (though not necessarily,
as has been lovingly claimed, his "first and foremost disciple" or "the true
inheritor of his eternal spiritual treasures")[1] and thus commanded, like him,
the status of both guru and saint. The widowed mother of the Udbodhan
household became the Holy Mother of the extended spiritual family, the
Ramakrishna Order. This dual role was not contradictory, because her spiritual reputation and status never conflicted with her maternal and mundane
concerns. This was possible because she was neither a brazen materialist
(though at times she was seen getting entangled with family problems and
even admonished for that)[2] nor an all-renouncing ascetic.

Sarada's maternal compassion and humility did not prevent her from
being stern and stubborn when necessary. Possessed of abundant common
sense, she was, to quote Satyen Majumdar, "affectionate but not feeble-
minded."[3] No doubt she was far from being a matriarch ruling the monastic
order with an iron hand. Yet her influence on the Ramakrishna Mission was
active, though covert. She was ever vigilant of any possible debasement of
the ideals of the order contingent upon expansion. The secretary of the
mission, Swami Saradananda, never even dared to do anything, however
trivial, without Mother's approval. The leaders of the order never ventured

to remonstrate against her objections or disagreements. At the same time, she did not hesitate to comply with others' decisions even when these appeared to contradict her personal beliefs and practices. Sometime in January 1901 Vivekananda visited Advaita Ashrama at Mayavati and was displeased to find some of his disciples worshiping Ramakrishna's photograph in contravention of the monastic rule against image worship. When the worshipers appealed to Sarada, she approved of the swami's stand wholeheartedly.[4]

II

She was quite forthright in declaring her own decisions. When some well-wishers of the mission advised the leaders to weed out nationalist revolutionaries from the order because of the vigilance of the secret police, she insisted:

> The Math has been established on the wishes of the Master. It is a heresy to transgress the rules of the order for fear of the displeasure of the government. Those who have become monks in Master's name will stay in the monastery, otherwise nobody else can. My boys will live under the tree but will never violate their vows.[5]

She was also quite firm in forcing Swami Keshavananda, head of the Koalpara Math, to reverse his decision to fire an incompetent cook.[6] In similar fashion she had stubbornly retained the services of a domestic hand accused of stealing and sacked by Vivekananda.[7] She also unhesitatingly cleansed a low-caste working woman from Mayapur village who, in a fit of malaria fever, had soiled her bed in sleep; she thus saved her from being reprimanded by people.[8] She came to the rescue of a young Brahmin widow accused of adultery and tormented by the villagers.[9] She was so moved by the performance of Tarasundari in the role of the Vaishnava devotee Ramanuja that she had little qualms about making the stage actress, a prostitute, sit on her lap, and she gave her an affectionate kiss of adoration and blessing.[10]

Her stubbornness was combined with an earthy pragmatism that often ran counter to monastic conventions and considerations. Thus, she did not hesitate to purchase foreign-made gifts for her near and dear ones, overriding the objections of her devotees who insisted on using homemade products. She even unequivocally told a young initiate that she regarded the English as her *children* also and so refused to give them up.[11] At the same time she reminded her devotee the schoolmaster Prabodh Chattopadhyay, who praised Western education and science as well as the material benefits of British administration: "But, my son, in spite of all those good deeds, our country is increasingly suffering from a dearth of food and clothing. We never suffered this much before."[12] When Swami Girijananda expressed his surprise at the news of the marriage of Sarada's teenage nephew Bhudev, she argued that those who are born in this world to enjoy should be free to do what pleased them. As she told Girijananda: "They have come for enjoyment, let them enjoy."[13] One of her disciples at Kother gave up consuming fish and meat when he found that Mother was a vegetarian. Sarada, however, persuaded him to resume his nonvegetarian habit by admonishing him: "Don't be foolish. I am asking you to eat fish and flesh."[14] While subscribing to the conventional belief that gurus always take upon themselves the sins of their disciples, she refused to bear the burden of others' sins throughout her life. For this reason she refused to give initiation in Baranasi (Kashi), a city believed to be a place where human actions remain forever indelible.[15] Yet she unhesitatingly agreed to perform *japa* daily on behalf of her disciple Surendra Bandyopadhyay, who was unable to do it on a regular basis.[16] In the elegant commentary of Bhumananda, "Ma actually demonstrated [her conviction] that all devotees belong to a race [or caste] of her own children."[17]

On occasions she would unhesitatingly and spontaneously exhibit natural human sentiments of frustration and fury. Though possessed of an extraordinary reserve of fortitude in coping with constant demands on her generosity from her relatives, Sarada would sometimes flare up. Once she exclaimed: "Listen, you, I seem to have blossomed as a lotus in a garbage dump—even the Master, too, was a lotus in a dunghill!"[18] Constantly under the watchful gaze of her devotees in Calcutta, Sarada longed for the relatively free country environment in which she had grown up. As she declared at her home, Jagadamba Ashrama: "This is our village. Koalpara is my living room. . . . Whenever I come here I'm able to move about freely. I feel a great relief after Calcutta. You people cage me there; I have to be careful all the time. I don't have to have anybody's permission for my movements in this part of the country."[19]

III

Though a mother to a community of monks and though she often counseled her young devotees against marriage because it "invites many complications," Sarada never totally opposed the idea of marriage. Once she complained about young men's reluctance to marry, and she told Susheela Mazumdar: "Ah, these days it has become a fashion with young men! Why can't a married man lead a virtuous life? It is through the mind that one

achieves everything. Didn't the Master marry me?" She even strongly recommended marriage for Mazumdar's son, and especially because he had
received initiation.[20] Likewise, even though she believed, *à la* Ramakrishna,
that one need not care for or be proud of the body, as it is nothing but a
pound of ash, she advised her visitor Mrinalini Devi to eat properly and to
nourish the body for the sake of performing *sadhan-bhajan*.[21] Once a woman
devotee questioned her inconsistent advice to people in respect of marriage—encouraging those inclined to a householder's life to marry as well
as advising others who sought an ascetic's career to renounce the world.
She gave a startlingly simple but sensible reply:

> Suppose a man has intense desire for enjoyment. Do you think he will
> listen to me, if I forbid him to enjoy that desire? Again, suppose a man, as
> a result of his many meritorious actions in past births, has understood all
> these as freaks of Maya and regards God as the only real thing. Should I not
> help him a little? Is there any end of suffering in this life of the world?[22]

Years before, during the active life of her husband, Sarada had blessed Bhu-
banmohini, the newlywed daughter of Ramakrishna's great patron, Balaram
Basu of Baghbazar. The young woman had insisted on visiting with Sarada
even on pain of becoming estranged from her husband. Sarada remarked:
"You are so devout at this [young] age! No, no, why should you renounce
[home]. Be happy with your husband and children."[23]

However, she was not used to hearing the problems of young devotees
trying to cope with feelings of lust. When a young man named Surendranath
Sarkar had the temerity to complain that "his heart was always restive and
he had no peace of mind because he could not get rid of carnal desires," the
Holy Mother, who had not experienced any sexuality in her own husband,
and who never counseled young men on their sexual problems, was perhaps stunned. As Surendra himself recalls, she responded with a silent gaze
(or rage?): "On hearing this Ma kept on staring at me for a long time,
saying nothing." The careless young man perhaps realized his faux pas and
hurriedly took leave of her. When he related his experience at Sarada's
place to SriM and wanted to know the meaning of Mother's behavior from
him, Gupta provided a spiritual hermeneutic, saying that Sarada's silent
stare was her divine gaze of grace *(kripadristi)*.[24]

IV

Several biographers of Sarada have wondered if her life can provide
any lesson for the modern Indian woman. Swami Mumukshananda has
admitted:

Even though Srima Saradadevi is the best exemplar of India's ancient ideals it is doubtful that the world of modern women would be able to accept her as the representative of the feminine ideals of the present or the future. Could the aspirations, the innermost yearnings, idealism, and the values of the women of the present age be satisfied by the Srima's ideals of life? It must be admitted that the time for the ideals she represented is long gone.

However, the same author has argued that both the traditional and the modern ideals of Indian life have a similar ultimate aim—to realize spiritual objectives: realization of the self, of God, truth, and liberation. Sarada's life manifested the fruition of these eternal goals of life and, with her serenity, stability, sincerity, and above all adaptability, she offers a link between tradition and modernity. "In fact," concludes the swami, "Srima Saradadevi's life offers a much needed corrective to the mad rush for liquidating spiritual treasures in the name of women's progress."[25]

Sarada's official biographer, Swami Gambhirananda, says the cultural significance of Sarada's life is that she serves as a model for the Indian women who, being misled by Western education, turned away from the natural and desirable course of authentic womanhood. While the swami concedes that "there is need for energizing our womanhood by drawing a little on foreign sources in order to make national life more vigorous and fruitful," he reminds readers that it would be harmful for India to forget her own pristine ideals.[26] Gambhirananda continues: "India eulogizes chastity and motherhood, since the ideal aimed at is a spiritual freedom which has for its foundation absolute self-control." Indian womanhood derives its inspiration from the Mother of the Universe and stands squarely upon such idealized figures as Sita, Savitri, and Damayanti. Sarada was an incarnation of the Divine Mother and "in her life the feminine virtues consequent on such positions in the family as daughter, sister, wife, or matron, reached their ideal states."[27] Hence her relevance in modern India.

Another scholar has detected in Sarada's life numerous strains of modernity. According to him, late colonial India appropriated the fundamental tenets of the European Enlightenment such as humanitarianism, globalism, individualism, strength of character, ability to cope with adverse circumstances, zest for life, resistance to injustice, progressivism, liberation of women, aesthetic and ecological sensibilities, nationalism and internationalism, and individual freedom and rights. And, as he argues, these characteristics were amply demonstrated in Sarada's life. Her sense of universal harmony is expressed in her remarks on the British: "They, too, are my children. . . . Everyone in the whole world is my child." She even called herself a mother of the animals.[28] Her character and conduct exemplify a wonderful combination of softness and sternness. Here we recall her stubborn stand in retaining the services of a domestic servant and a cook sacked by senior monks.[29] She similarly severely chided a neighbor who was thrashing his wife and rescued the helpless woman from torture.[30]

Sarada wanted women to be educated and self-reliant. When one of her female devotees lamented over her inability to get her daughter married, Sarada advised: "Why worry if you fail to get her married? Send her to Nivedita's school. She will learn and be happy."[31] Sarada wanted to be well-informed about her world. She advised the girls of Nivedita's school at Bosepara Lane: "My children, always try to observe what is going on around you wherever you go. Try to get as much information as you can about the place you stay, but do not talk about it to others."[32] She used to encourage the monastic initiates *(brahmacharis)* to learn English so that they could exchange ideas with Westerners. She even appointed an English teacher for them.[33] She was equally fun-loving and humorous. She enjoyed the funny cavorting and romping of a mature adult, Dr. Jnanedranath Kanjilal, even when it was objected to by a *brahmachari* with refined manners.[34] She once noticed that her devotee children were not as eager for *prasada* (sacred food, that is, food dedicated to God) as usual because her meal that day consisted of mere barley due to her illness. She quipped: "What happened, you aren't showing your devotion to my *prasada* today!"[35]

Her liberal outlook on life even led her to defy the traditional fetishes of purity and casteism. She found little problem in dining with foreigners.[36] "Who is a sudra, Golap?" she asked her companion Golap-ma. "Devotees have no caste."[37] Her generosity and compassion touched nearly everyone. As she remarked once: "I wish to feed everybody in one plate. However, this wretched land boasts casteism." When one of her devotees objected to Sarada's accepting a gift from a man reported to be guilty of stealing, she became angry and quipped: " I know who's good and who's bad. Human beings err often. How many care to strive to improve them?"[38] She likewise showed her maternal affection to her so-called *dakat-baba* and to a notorious Muslim bandit named Amzad. "Amzad is as truly my son as my Sarat [Saradananda] himself is," Sarada declared unhesitatingly.[39]

In a similarly independent spirit, at Kothar, sometime in December 1910, she had a brahmin Christian convert reconverted to Hinduism and then initiated. She deliberately invited a low-caste devotee into her room, and when he hesitated to comply, pointing out his social status, she admonished him: "Who says you're from a low caste? You're my son—come in and take a seat."[40] Her palanquin carrier *(palki behara)*, Yogindra Das, a.k.a Yoge Dule *(dules* belonged to a low social caste who by occupation were palanquin carriers), was like her own junior brother, and had free access to Sarada's house. As his son Shantiram recalled in his later years:

Golap-ma (Golapsundari Devi, d. 1924)

In those days, we did not have the right to enter the area beneath the thatched roof of the brahmin's home. Even the brahmins of Jairambati used to keep a distance from our touch. But we had free access to our aunt [Sarada]. She blessed us by touching our head. She fed low-caste people herself and even scraped off their bowls after their meals. She was threatened with excommunication by the village elders and even fined by them. But she didn't care. She was no ordinary human being. Everything about her was different.[41]

V

In the end, however, one must recognize that Saradamani was neither an ascetic nor a saint in conventional Hindu terms. She was not a *brahmacharini,* who is usually initiated formally into a tradition of asceticism by a recognized guru through a ritual commitment to a particular path to salvation by rejecting the life of a householder. Yet, true to the Hindu tradition, textual as well as cultural, she followed her *stridharma* (feminine duties), and thus all her religious duties were marked primarily by her constant care for the comfort and happiness of her charges.[42] A true Hindu woman, Sarada's life reflects the triumph of essential feminine altruism as well as materialistic concerns. Though the Holy Mother of an ascetic order, she remained very much of this world and in this world. Her life demonstrates a wonderful harmony of materiality and spirituality—of *bhuma* (the sublime) and *bhumi* (the mundane).

Saradamani, in fact, lived a comfortable though busy life surrounded by maids and cooks and innumerable devotees always eager to lend a hand in any chore. Swami Arupananda even provides interesting information on her favorite snacks and beverages.[43] She would often request her devotees to cook a favorite dish for her. When jestingly reminded by a devotee that she made her devotees take the trouble of cooking for her, the Holy Mother confessed with disarming candor: "Why shouldn't I ask for food of my daughters? Isn't it my good fortune? What do you say, my child?"[44] She was also not a typical married female saint—one whose *prapattibhakti* (single-minded devotion to God and total dedication to God's service) replaced her *pati* (husband) with an *istadebata* (chosen ideal).[45] Like other Hindu women of her day, Sarada regarded her husband as her lord and master, and even more so after he nad been transformed into a popular *paramahamsa.* As his widow, she continued to regard him as her guru and god. In fact, contemporary accounts are silent as to her professed attachment to any male deity unconnected with Sri Ramakrishna. At the same time, she was not a typical female ascetic who deliberately espouses renunciation by turning her back on the values of marriage—that is, *stridharma* or *swadharma* (true duties)—and thus discovers a way to rebel against society's norms and injunctions. Sarada, the Holy Mother, who was in fact a practicing guru of numerous devotees and disciples, does not fit the profile of some female ascetics and gurus of Baranasi discussed in an interesting study written some years ago.[46]

VI

Sarada's *sannyasi* biographers have proclaimed that she was mentored and prepared for her divine and maternal role by her *paramahamsa* husband. It would be instructive to have some idea of the construction of Saradamani's divine motherhood in the hagiographical literature. Among numerous studies, perhaps the one by Swami Budhananda is the most incisive and insistent. The swami writes that though Sri Ramakrishna was an untidy and eccentric man *(elomelo),* he was meticulous in bringing up the young Sarada. He had proclaimed her to the world on his own initiative and in his own glory. Especially toward the end of his life, when he was afflicted with terminal cancer, the Master drew his wife onto the center stage of his divine play with consummate dexterity. One day at Kashipur (where Ramakrishna had relocated for the treatment of his disease) he kept staring at her. When Sarada inquired if he was intending to say something to her, he said in a complaining tone: "Listen, my dear, aren't you going to do something? . . . Will this one alone be doing everything all by himself?" The Holy Mother realized her own helpless state and responded: "I am a woman, what could I do?" He retorted instantly: "Not so. You've got to do a lot." At another time in his ecstatic mood Ramakrishna said to his wife: "Look how the people of Calcutta are crawling around like worms in the dark. Please look after them." On her own admission, Ramakrishna appeared to his wife in a dream after his death and said: "No, you better stay back. There are many things to be done." According to Budhananda, the Master not only handed over to her the responsibilities for bringing all his unfinished projects to completion, but even imparted numerous mantras to carry on his mission. Sarada thus received her divine husband's imprimatur to work for saving human souls.[47] And she did it with great success, because she was endowed by the late *paramahamsa* with divinity. It is thus clear that Saradamani's monastic biographers recognized her divinity and accorded her their loyalty and love by privileging the intentions and ingenuity of her God-man husband. Even Sarada herself admitted to a devotee that the Master left her with the responsibility for manifesting maternal power *(matribhava).*[48]

The most influential theological (and, by the same token, the most patriarchal) argument for the Holy Mother's divinity comes from Gambhira-nanda. According to him, divine incarnation is the work of God in conjunction with his "Power," that is, *shakti*. The divine descent *(avatarana >avatara)* is accompanied by *shakti* as is evidenced by "the descent of Sita with Ramachandra, Sri Radhika with Krishna, Jasodhara with Buddha, and Vishnupriya with Sri Chaitanya." The swami cites the authority of Ramakrishna's official biographer, Saradananda, who had posited that the goddess Kali, the deity who dances on the prostrate body of Shiva and who promises blessing and protection while wearing at the same time a necklace of heads, is the perfect representation of the eternal association of Power with Consciousness (Absolute Brahman) whom the rishis of India worshiped.[49] Quoting from the *Chandi,* which has her incarnate for the same reasons as God does in the *Bhagavad Gita,* that is, for eradicating evil, Gambhirananda provides Saradamani's divine raison d'être. The goddess incarnated as the Holy Mother because of "the conflict on the psychological plane in the modern age," which is a greater evil "than the old mythological war between the gods and the demons."[50] Thus, according to the monastic exegesis of the Holy Mother's *lila* (divine play), Saradamani is the incarnation of the *shakti* (or spouse) of the Absolute Brahman, the divine *purusa*, who is Sri Ramakrishna. In other words, Sarada's divinity is predicated upon that of her husband as, undoubtedly, is her status in the Ramakrishna Order as the widow of the *paramahamsa*, the guru figure after whom the order is named.

VII

Though admittedly Sarada's married and widowed life in a patriarchal society was guided by the admonition and approbation of males—by her husband, who had instructed her on *stridharma* and even frightened her about becoming a biological mother, as well as by her devotees, who unabashedly declared her divinity—she was a far from passive recipient of the dictates of her culture and society. On the contrary, she was resourceful enough to discover sources of empowerment in her conformity to and compromise with tradition.[51] The teachings of her husband—a semiliterate brahmin male from an agrarian society—on women, family, and livelihood were appropriated by his male devotees because he legitimized through his dicta on *kamini-kanchana* their fears and anxieties in respect to females at home and to foreign masters outside the home.[52] The *paramahamsa* also appealed to women, mostly housewives (the only exception being the socially ostracized stage actress Nati Binodini), because they had internalized the ethos of their patriarchal culture. Sarada, on the other hand, gained a following by playing the role of a perfect mother of the household and by catering to and counseling men and women on behavior considered proper by the *bhadralok* culture of Bengal. She acted as mother to her spiritual family by acknowledging the undying influence of the spiritual father, her husband. Her reassuring message to a visitor toward the end of her life was: "Fear not, my son, you ought to know that the Master is always looking after you. I am here–have no cause for alarm as long as I'm present as your mother."[53] Bandyopadhyay rightly suggests that Sarada's character was molded by the traditional domesticity of agrarian Bengal. As a married woman she was the bastion of tradition, while at the same time as a true *sahadharmini* ("helpmate" in Nikhilananda's translation) she became a prop for her husband's world outside of the home. Sarada thus took over the nurturing responsibilities of her *paramahamsa* spouse's ever-widening circle of devotees, disciples, and admirers and thus became heir to the leadership of the Ramakrishna Order as the *sanghajanani*.[54]

In a wonderful way, Sarada's unrequited motherhood enabled her to achieve prominence in public life as the mother figure of the Ramakrishna Order. Had she been an actual biological mother of a son or a daughter, she would probably not have come close to her husband's flock. Her life would have been spent as a widow dependent on the goodwill and care of her children, who would have been busy with their own families. Sarada's life would have remained obscure at best or uncomfortable at worst. Swami Bhumananda has reminded his readers of the extremely precarious life of a Hindu widow in nineteenth-century Bengal.[55] Moreover, as a biological mother, she would not have been able to shower so much extraordinary love on her devotees and disciples. In any case, Sarada's sterling success as a public mother without being a biological *mother* was possible only in the sociocultural environment of Bengal. The Bengali familial and social ethos pivots around the idealized maternal figure who is a sustainer of life by providing compassion and cooking. Food in a Bengali household occupies a quasi-spiritual space in that it not only enhances life but also ingratiates the devotee to his god, thereby acting as a sacred sacrifice or offering *(prasada)*. The mother of the household is the provider of food—she is the veritable real-life goddess Annapurna and Lakshmi combined. Sarada fit the bill perfectly, and thus she was what Chitrita Banerji calls a goddess in her elegant essay on the culinary culture of Bengal.[56]

VIII

Arguably, Sarada's life may not have much appeal to Western women, whose acute egalitarianism and determined struggle for equality with men will find her submission to tradition quite archaic. Though Western feminism finds the archetype of the Hindu goddess quite valuable as a model, she is the product of a frankly patriarchal society. Moreover, such domesticated feminine goddesses as Lakshmi or Parvati have little use for Western feminists, who discovered a model in the goddess Kali, representing an autonomous force that subverts the masculinist norm and authority.[57] It is doubtful if Sarada, who was often worshiped as Kali and who often thought of herself as the incarnation of the Magna Mater, would have been comfortable in emulating the goddess's fierce independence and power. Like a typical Bengali widow of her time, Saradamani internalized the cultural dictates of her society and could neither think nor act in any socially subversive way, though, as has been noted earlier, she did on rare occasions exhibit some measure of independent judgment.

Yet her life was neither a pale shadow of that of her famous husband nor a repudiation of her society's norms, but a testimony to her spontaneous ability to make it meaningful and praiseworthy. She did possess an enormous reserve of liberality and pragmatism, and she could be considered as a reformer from within. She represents the Bengali paradigm of the Great Goddess, the magnanimous mother. Hence Sarada's odyssey possesses a potential in her own country, and it really is irrelevant if she fails to inspire modern women seeking political power, social equality, and personal meaning in a world still hierarchically gendered.[58] However, as a scholar has argued, a "feminist religion" countering the "masculist materialism" of "patriarchal religion" is likely to create new myths while attempting to demolish the old ones. A balanced approach and a more wholesome option for our world would be, it has been suggested, a "universal religion," which conduces to the development of a "perfect personality" of the individual seeking to realize the "divine principle" in everybody.[59] In many respects, Saradamani appears to be a true exemplar of this balanced personality. This is perhaps one of the reasons that she exercises a quiet and gentle influence on some westerners. As one of her American devotees declared, "In the West we are conditioned to admire that which is big, spectacular and instantaneous. This kind of conditioning can also influence our attitude to spiritual life if we are not careful. In spiritual life it is the apparently little things that count and the Holy Mother emphasized this point very much." The devotee concluded confidently:

> Outwardly the Holy Mother's influence in the West has been exercised through her role as the support and complement to the life of Sri Ramakrishna. But at a deeper spiritual level she has exercised a direct, personal influence on the mind of many westerners through her self-giving, all-accepting, easily approachable and accessible motherhood on the one hand and her immense practicality and robust common sense on the other.[60]

Sarada's life suggests an important dimension of women's struggle for identity and leadership in the colonial society of late-nineteenth-century Bengal by an affirmation of the visions and values of the urban middle class mediated through the rhetoric of religion. Sarada did not possess Ramakrishna's charisma or charm. While he stole the heart of his devotees by his unique repertoire—dances, trances, songs, sermons, and sheer mischievousness—she endeared herself by the maternal compassion expressed through the hard work of cooking and catering. She neither sang nor preached (she in fact considered lecturing as preeminently a male prerogative)[61] nor even amused others with witty repartee, but simply delighted in mothering her devotees and disciples. Also, not being educated and not hailing from the *bhadralok* class—that is, not being a *bhadramahila* (lady) in the strict sense of the term—Sarada never fully shared the latter's ideal of a class- and caste-conscious genteel woman. Moreover, being somewhat free from the typical brahmanical caste bias, she had little difficulty socializing with lower-caste or lower-class people, the so-called *itarjan*.[62] Yet, Sarada the compassionate mother exercised a powerful appeal for Indian, especially Bengali, men. In fact, as Shivanath Shastri has written, the great luminaries of Bengal had received their first lesson in philanthropy after having experienced personally the spontaneous love and affection from women.[63] Pandit Ishwarchandra Vidyasagar (1820–91), who had been a beneficiary of the care and compassion of his schoolmate's mother Raimani Devi, in Calcutta, and who struggled to legalize widow-marriage, confessed: "Many people point out my partiality for women. I think this accusation is justified. One who has experienced Raimani's humility and humanity and yet remains indifferent to women's interests will find none in this world equal to him in ingratitude and iniquity."[64] Sarada's maternal appeal is also recognized by a professional woman of modern Calcutta:

In the history of nineteenth-century Bengal I do not revere or adore a woman more than Holy Mother. Her gentleness, her clear-eyed perceptions of essential truths, her indomitable quiet strength which she drew from her inner spiritual resources, her ability to reach out to people, and her genuineness make her a unique personality–all the more so because she lived in a society where women had no separate identity and were treated with neglect and regarded as morally and intellectually inferior to men.[65]

IX

Herein lies the significance of her odyssey—the remarkable story of how a Cinderella became, literally, the prima donna of a preeminently male monastic order. Though, admittedly, Sarada's primacy in the order was facilitated

Saradamani and Margaret Noble (Sister Nivedita, 1867–1911)

by the cultural conditioning of the Indian males who, unlike their Western counterparts, easily accepted women in leadership positions, this rustic woman, on her part, had appropriated most of the values of the urban middle class and reinforced them by her counsel and care for those who came to her either from within the city or from the suburbs.[66] She conscientiously upheld the socially approved norms of femininity and thus was quite critical of unruly behavior on the part of women. She was so convinced of the propriety of covering women's bodies that she would consider a woman virtually naked if she lifted her sari up to the knees. At Udbodhan during her terminal illness, a monk came to see her and upon entering her room found her asleep. He rubbed her feet reverentially. At the time her head was uncovered. After he had left Sarada rebuked her attendant devotee Saralabala (later Pravrajika Bharatiprana) for not having drawn the veil to cover her head.[67] She even unhesitatingly defied her husband's counsel to women to be rid of the three impediments to the realization of God—shame, hate, and fear *(lajja, ghrina, bhai, tin thakte nai)*—and argued that the Master's dicta were not meant for lay people but for those who were experiencing divine madness.[68]

Chetna Mandavia has amply documented the Holy Mother's "practicality and managerial ability" in her personal life and public life (which were often inseparable). Mandavia has further illustrated Sarada's progressive and liberal outlook, her amicable relationships with Sister Nivedita, Sarah Bull, and Josephine MacLeod—Swami Vivekananda's Western disciples.[69] Nivedita, who first encountered Sarada in the winter of 1898, shrewdly observed that though Sarada was not fully literate—she could barely read and not write at all—"it is not to be supposed that she is an uneducated woman." The sister especially admired "the stateliness of her courtesy and her great open mind," which was "almost as wonderful as her sainthood."[70] Yet we must note that Sarada was cautious about defying the prevailing prejudices of her rural society. For example, she prevented Nivedita from visiting Jairambati, both not to embarrass her foreign devotee and not to offend her caste-conscious village neighbors. "No dear, while I am alive you should not go there." the Holy Mother entreated the sister. "If you do, they will out-caste me."[71]

Saradamani's pragmatism and piety have been wonderfully captured by Gambhirananda, whose passionate plea for the need to understand Saramani's achievement is as elegant as it is eloquent. According to him, the Holy Mother's life was anchored deeply in the complicated mundane problems of domestic life, which is full of tears, tribulations, and torments. Yet her grace transcended all the degradation and vexation of mundane concerns. As the swami concludes,

[T]his interfusion of divine and human elements makes the Mother's life instructive and its appeal irresistible to men who tread the wonted paths of the work-a-day world, and inspiring and illuminating to others who are in search of a higher ideal. And in particular, her life is of special significance to women who spend their lives with their families in a more real sense than men do.[72]

Swami Nikhilananda has compared Saradamani to a number of historical women. She has been compared to the twelfth-century south Indian mystic Godai, popularly known as Andal. She is also compared to another south Indian woman, the thirteenth-century princess of Warangel, Rudramba. Additionally, Sarada is seen as a true successor of the heroic royal nurse of Rajputana, Panna, who let her own child die at the hands of the Muslim marauders looking for the royal infant. Likewise, Sarada is compared to the queen of Mewar, Padmini, who immolated herself to protect her chastity from the lustful Alaudddin Khilji. Mirabai, the sixteenth-century widow of the heir-presumptive of Mewar, and Ahalyabai, daughter of the Maratha chieftain of the eighteenth century, have also been seen as worthy precursors of the Holy Mother. Nikhilananda has also compared Sarada to such epic personalities as Savitri and Gandhari of the *Mahabharata* and Sita, "the paragon of all the women mentioned in the epics," of the *Ramayana*, and even to such scriptural figures as Maitreyi, the intellectual spouse of the philosopher Yajnavalkya, in the *Brihadaranyaka Upanisad*.[73] Most interestingly, Nikhilananda has accorded Sarojini Naidu (1879–1949)—a younger contemporary of Sarada's, the first woman president of the Indian National Congress, and later the first woman governor of state (Uttar Pradesh) of independent India—pride of place as the first female figure to be compared to the Holy Mother.[74] In short, Nikhilananda claims Sarada to be the representative of Indian womanhood of all ages.

Nevertheless, in the estimation of the present writer, the religious women whose character and conduct could be compared favorably with Sarada's are in fact three, from Maharastra, Uttar Pradesh, and Bengal, respectively. The Maharastrian housewife and saint of the seventeenth century, Bahina Bai, had declared: "She who conducts her household duties and her religious life equally—only she catches the heavens."[75] Sarada's personal outlook on *pravritti* (her social role and responsibilities) and *nivritti* (her absorption in God) shows an uncanny resemblance to Bahina's views. Similarly, Sarada resembles two of her famous successors: the currently active Anand Mata of Haridwar who exhibits a tough earthy pragmatism and exudes quiet authority in a male dominated *ashrama,* and the ascetic housewife of Bengal born a generation later after Sarada, Nirmala Sundari Bhattacharya, who achieved celebrity as Anandamayi Ma (Blissful Mother) in postcolonial India. Though, admittedly, both Anandamayi Ma and Anand

Mata are more modern in their outlook—for example, they advocate women's spiritual equality with men—they, like Sarada, upheld all the norms of their patriarchal society and emerged as religious leaders with a considerable following in India. Especially Anandamayi, like Sarada, elicited undying love and loyalty from her devotees. What a female devotee of Anandamayi Ma said of her guru could easily apply to her great forbear:

> Ma is my Mother, my God incarnate, and therefore, my association with her, my recognition of her, will carry me to rest with her eternally. I need only sit in the lap of Mother to have it all, both worldly and spiritual fulfillment.[76]

In many respects, too, Sarada resembled closely her older contemporary Sharadasundari, mother of the famous Brahmo leader Keshabchandra Sen (1838–84), "who had lived within the confines of the *antahpur* . . . [and] . . . displayed a remarkable degree of flexibility, tenacity and a spirit of adventure. . . ."[77] Though Saradamani harbored several progressive values and attitudes—most remarkably her indifference to casteism in contradistinction to her caste-conscious husband—she ultimately became a part of the urban moral universe that remained anchored, in spite of colonial influence or precisely because of it, in the traditional ethos of Hindu India.[78] There is a kernel of truth in Gambhirananda's assessment of the relevance of Sarada's odyssey for modern times. Through the haze of the swami's hagiographical exuberance the basic point is made clear that the Holy Mother was no dazzling spiritual personality noted for erudition, eloquence, or energy, but was a quiet, though unmistakable, exemplar of the best of human ideals.[79] In the end, Sarada's glory is grounded in her humanity. With her purity and piety tempered with pragmatism, Saradamani, a *mater dolorosa* par excellence, was not only like the Hindu Mother Goddess, "Mother who is not a mother,"[80] but, to borrow Jaroslav Pelikan's felicitous description of the Virgin Mary, a "woman for all seasons—and all reasons."[81]

Glossary

abhayamudra: an iconic mudra depicting the gesture of protection; the right hand is slightly elevated and upturned with the palm facing forward and the fingers raised.

antahpur: inner apartments of the house.

babu: the designation for a Bengali urban middle-class male employed as a clerk in a British office in colonial India. It is considered a pejorative term for colonial males given by the imperial powers.

Bagala: or Bagalamukhi, the "Crane-Faced," is one of the ten tantric goddesses known as *mahavidyas*. Bagala is "the paralyzer" of demons.

bhadralok: the genteel class of the middle stratum of the society of colonial Bengal.

bhadramahila: feminine form of *bhadralok* (q.v.).

Bhagavati: feminine form of Bhagavan or God. Also another name of the Mother Goddess.

bhairavi: a female ritualistic practitioner of the tantra (q.v.). Bhairavi, with a capital *B,* is also one of the ten *mahavidyas* and depicted as "the Fierce One."

bhakti: devotion.

bhava: literally "mood" but in the mystic literature standing for "spiritual mood."

Brahma: the creator god, the first person of the Hindu trinity, of which the other two persons are Vishnu (q.v.) and Shiva (q.v.).

brahmachari: a monastic initiate who has taken the vows of celibacy, poverty, nonviolence, and the like.

brahmacharini: feminine form of *brahmachari* (q.v.).

Brahman: the Absolute or the Supreme Reality of Vedic philosophy.

deshamata: motherland or the Mother Goddess of the land—a nationalistic image of colonial India.

devi: goddess.

dhutura: or *datura* in Latin, a name for a thorny, bitter, and poisonous fruit usually used in Shiva (q.v.) worship.

diksha: initiation required in various walks of Hindu life from the rites of passage

114

to entry into a religious creed. There are various forms of *diksha*, the two principal kinds being Vedic and tantric.

divyonmada: divinely mad individual. Also designating divine madness, which is regarded as the highest state of *prapattibhakti* (q.v.) in Vaishnava (q.v.) tradition.

Durga: the ten-handed and lion-borne warrior goddess, an incarnation of the Mother Goddess, worshiped throughout India but most popularly in Bengal.

guru: spiritual mentor.

gurubhai: brother disciple of the same spiritual cohort under the same guru.

istadevata: a chosen divine ideal or a personal deity.

Ishwara: "Lord," the Supreme Being creating, maintaining, and annihilating the world and the only principle of comprehension and attainment of grace through bhakti (q.v.) according to all theistic systems of Hindu India.

Ishwari: feminine form of Ishwara (q.v.).

Jagaddhatri: upholder of the world," an incarnation of the Mother Goddess as a four-handed lion-borne deity.

Jagajjanani: "Mother of the Universe," an appellation of the Mother Goddess.

japa: counting beads or the name of a chosen deity to achieve concentration during meditation.

Kali: also known as Jagajjanani (q.v.), Kali (literally meaning a "black female") represents Shakti (q.v.) and is worshiped as Shiva's (q.v.) consort. She also manifests, like Shiva, a dual nature: benign and bizarre.

kamini-kanchana: literally meaning "woman and gold (or wealth)" but standing as a metaphor for lust and lure. Ramakrishna popularized the phrase in his numerous sermons on the absolute necessity of discarding woman and wealth on the part of a spiritual aspirant.

Krishna: popular Hindu folk god, believed to be an incarnation of Vishnu (q.v.) in the guise of a dark-skinned cowherd playboy.

Ma Anandamayi: also styled as "Anandamayi Ma" and meaning, literally, "Blissful Mother," one of the popular appellations for Kali in Bengal. Also the monastic name of Nirmala Sundari Bhattacharya, a Bengali mystic woman (1896–1982).

madhura bhava: literally meaning "sweet mood" but representing the Vaishnava (q.v.) devotional practice in which the male adept regards himself as a female lover of God, the divine male.

maya: illusion.

pan: betel leaf seasoned with lime paste and catechu *(acacia)* chewed as a mouth refresher.

panchatapa: a ritual of penance usually undertaken by a Bengali Hindu woman for seven days, during which she sits within a circle of lighted mounds of cow dung cakes, meditating and performing *japa* (q.v.) with a view to ridding herself of unwanted desires.

pandit: a scholar or a pedant.

paramahamsa: literally means "supreme swan" but designating "great embodied soul" (or *jiva*). The word has been in use since the first century C.E. The word *hamsa* (meaning "swan") represents the supreme *(parama)* essence or one who has realized that essence.

prakriti: literally meaning "nature," a designation for the ultimate cause of the phenomenal material world, which is an unintelligent and unconscious principle, uncaused, eternal, and all-pervading. It is the primordial matter or substance, often conceived as a female principle.

prapattibhakti: devotion of total surrender to God.

prasada: sacred food offered to the gods and believed to be leftover from divine consumption.

puja: ritual worship.

purana: the *puranas* or "antiquities" are versified texts containing details of the creation of the world, the genealogy of the gods, human prehistory, and royal dynasties. The texts originated at the beginning of the Christian era and were added up to the tenth century and even later. There are eighteen principal *puranas* and a great number of secondary *puranas*.

Radha: the milkmaid *(gopi)* lover of Krishna according to Hindu folklore; as interpreted theologically by the Vaishnavas, she represents the supreme example of *prapattibhakti* (q.v.).

Rama: a folk god of the Hindus, like Krishna, widely worshipped throughout India, especially in the northern part of the country.

Ramlala: a doll of Rama (q.v.) showing the god as a child, somewhat comparable to Gopala, the child form of Krishna.

ruti: Bengali for the Hindi *roti* or *chapati*, that is, a round, unleavened wheat bread much like the Mexican tortilla.

sadhan-bhajan: procedure of ritual worship accompanied by devotional songs.

sadhana: procedure of worship for the invocation of the gods. It is used as a general term for spiritual exercise.

samadhi: a superconscious state or an ecstatic state or syncope.

sannyasi: ascetic or monk.

sannyasini: fem. form of *sannyasi*.

Saraswati: the goddess of learning, the Hindu Minerva.

Shakta: followers of the goddess Shakti and also a sect of Tantrikas.

Shakti: the cosmic energizing principle worshiped as the Mother Goddess; the worship originated, perhaps, in the non-Aryan culture of the Indus Valley. In the Vedic tradition, Shakti connotes the power of Brahman (q.v.) conceived as the female principle through which the manifestations of the universe are effected. Mythologically, Shakti is equated with the goddess Kali (q.v.) or Parvati (the domesticated form of Durga as Shiva's spouse).

Shaiva: a sect of Tantrikas who are worshippers of Shiva (q.v.).

Shiva: also known as Maheshwara or Mahadeva ("Great God"), one person of the Hindu trinity, the other two persons being Brahma (q.v.) and Vishnu (q.v.). In the *puranas* (q.v.) Shiva is the benign aspect of the Vedic god Rudra (the god of destruction).

sodashi puja: literally, worship of a sixteen-year-old girl. The goddess Sodashi, otherwise known as Tripurasundari or Srividya, is the beautiful maiden form of the Mother Goddess. The worship of the Mother Goddess in human form is sanctioned by the scriptures, especially the tantra (q.v.), though the usual objects of devotion are pictures, pitchers *(ghata),* clay images *(pratima),* or *yantras* (ritualistic drawings).

sridharma: duties of an ideal Hindu wife.

swadharma: scripturally sanctioned true duties of various categories of people.

tantra: system of religious philosophy in which Shiva, Vishnu, or the Divine Mother is the Ultimate Reality, differentiated, respectively, as Shaiva (q.v.), Vaishnava, and Shakta (q.v.) Tantra. Also means the scriptures dealing with these philosophies.

Vaishnava: a sect of Vishnu (q.v.) worshipers and generally the followers of Sri Chaitanya (1485–1534) in Bengal and of Ramanuja (1017–1137) and Madhva (1199–1278) in southern India.

vatsalya bhava: mood of maternal affection for God regarded as a child.

Vishnu: one person of the Hindu trinity the god of cosmic order and sustenance.

Vishwajanani: "Mother of the Universe," an appellation of the Mother Goddess.

yoga: literally meaning "yoke" or "union," designating the Hindu philosophy postulating union of the individual soul *(jiva* or *atman)* with the Universal (or Supreme) Soul *(paramatman).* The word is also used to designate the methods by which to realize this union.

Appendix A:
Holy Mother's *Logia:* A Selection

The Western woman will learn from the contemplation of the Holy Mother's life, that to be the equal of man, or to command his respect, she does not have to imitate man's adventure or to enter into a fierce competition with him in all fields of life.

—Swami Nikhilananda

"Listen, my son, what is there to fear? The world is full of mirth as well as misery. You do not have to be afraid. Let terror and temptation haunt you, but what could these do to you? You have nothing to fear. My son, bear in mind at all times: 'I have a mother'."[1]

"One must speak the truth even when it is unpleasant."[2]

"Lack of shame or restraint, especially on the part of women, may degenerate into prolixity."[3]

"Women should not indulge in excesses [*badabadi*]. They have to be careful and mindful of their dignity in their movements and behavior. As they say, a woman wearing a twenty-foot-long cloth is virtually naked if it exposes her knees."[4]

"There is no virtue greater than patience, and there are no treasures equal to satisfaction."[5]

"Start eating fish from tomorrow. Otherwise you will not be cured of diarrhea and will become progressively more weak."[6]

"Indeed, I have some gems of brothers. They must have practiced cutthroat austerity [*galakata tapasya*]. Maybe that's why I am stuck to this world. I have never experienced so much agitation as well as attachment!"[7]

"People often make mistakes. But how many know how to correct them?"[8]

"I feel like feeding everyone from the same plate. But this wretched country of ours harbors caste discrimination."[9]

"Look, practicing discrimination, meditation, contemplation, or trying to dispel doubts about things—all this is for purifying the mind by detaching it from distractions and impermanent stuff with a view to become eager for His company."[10]

"People never care to probe their own heart but find faults of others. If they see their own shortcomings and strive to overcome them, they won't need to pick on others."[11]

"One man performs severe austerities throughout his life to realize God, but does not succeed, whereas another man gets his realization practically without any effort. It depends upon the grace of God."[12]

"[M]isery is only the gift of God. It is the symbol of His compassion."[13]

"[T]he difference between a great soul and an ordinary man is this: The latter weeps while leaving the body, whereas the former laughs. Death seems to him a mere play."[14]

"A monk is like a bleached cloth, and the householder is like a black one. One does not notice the spots in a black cloth so much, but even a drop of ink looks so prominent on white linen."[15]

"Do you know, my son, that the Master had a motherly affection for everybody? He has left me here to awaken maternal feeling in the world."[16]

Even the guru must be told the plain truth. There's no harm in it."[17]

"You must work, work frees you from the fetters of work, and this results in detachment. One must not stay away from work."[18]

"Only humans could become God. Everything is possible through right action."[19]

"Come in, my child. You now realize that you've sinned and you repent for that. I'll initiate you. Place everything at the Master's feet and have no fear."[20]

"Mind is like a crazy elephant. It runs like wind. That's why you must use your discretion in everything and work indefatigably for realizing the divine."[21]

"Even the moon has spots. May my heart have none."[22]

"Love is our only real treasure. His family [i.e., the Ramakrishna Order] is built upon love."[23]

"On attaining real knowledge one only sees Mother all around him—gods and stuff [ishwar-tishwar] vanish. Everything merges into One."[24]

"As flower or sandalwood emit aroma when touched and smelt or rubbed, so real knowledge follows a discourse on God. However, you will realize true knowledge instantly if you give up all desires."[25]

"How will you understand the sufferings of a miserable wretch? You aren't a mother."[26]

"What else shall you do if you do not believe in the words of high-souled men? Is there any other way except the one trodden by sages and seers and other holy men?"[27]

"Be content in all circumstances and take His name."[28]

"The Master is really God who assumed human body to remove the sufferings of men. He moved about just as a king walks through his city in disguise, and he left the world as soon as his identity was discovered."[29]

"Householders need not have external renunciation. Internal renunciation will come to them of itself."[30]

"I am a woman, and I follow my womanly nature."[31]

"Look, do not try to start a sensation by shouting vande mataram ["hail mother"]. Rather you should make looms and weave cloth. I wish to spin thread if I can get a spinning wheel. Do constructive work."[32]

"Son, it is Nature's law, just as you find the full moon and the new moon. Similarly the mind is possessed of noble thoughts at times, and haunted by evil thoughts at other moments."[33]

"In earlier days I also had an eye for people's faults. Thereafter I wept and wept before the Master, praying, 'O Master! I do not wish to see any one's faults' and finally got rid of that habit. You might have done good to a man a thousand times and harm only once; he will turn away from you for that one offence. People see only the faults. One should in fact note the merits."[34]

"However much of Japa you do, however much of work you perform, all is for nothing. If Mahamaya does not open the way, is anything possible for any one? Oh bound soul! Surrender, surrender. Then alone will She take compassion on you and leave your path open."[35]

"You need not entertain any fear. I say, in the Kali Yuga the mental commission of a sin is no sin at all. Free your mind from all such worries. You have nothing to fear."[36]

"Admittedly, the guru's words and commands are the ultimate authority in spiritual matters, but in mundane affairs you ought to decide on your course of action after giving due consideration to what is beneficial."[37]

To a devotee who wished to transfer Sarada's rheumatism unto himself by magical means the Holy Mother said: "No, no, my child, please don't do that. You perhaps don't know that this [affliction] will pain me a lot more if it attacks you–my condition will deteriorate terribly [*goder upar visphoda habey*] because I am your mother."[38]

"Let me tell you something. If you seek peace, my child, never find faults of anyone. Always blame yourself. Learn to make the world your own. Nobody is a stranger. The whole world is your own."[39]

Appendix B:
Select Biographical Abstracts

Abhedananda, Swami (1866–1939): monastic name of Kaliprasanna Chandra, who had been a young devotee and was later a disciple of Ramakrishna. He was a Vedanta enthusiast and hence nicknamed Kali Vedanti by his monastic brethren. He later became a disciple of the Holy Mother. He lectured in London for some months in 1896 and thereafter spent several years in the United States.

Adbhutananda, Swami (d. 1920): monastic name of Rakhturam, a native of Bihar. He had been part of the domestic help in the household of Ramchandra Datta and later became a devotee of Ramakrishna. He was nicknamed Latu (or Leto) by the Master. Illiterate but extremely devoted to Sarada and kindhearted, the swami was admired and loved by all his brother monks as well as by friends and acquaintances.

Basu, Balaram (1842–90): Ramakrishna's householder disciple and a wealthy Bengali landlord of Kothar (Orissa). He became one of the Master's *rasaddars* (supplier of victuals) and was noted for his generosity toward all devotees, disciples, and admirers of Ramakrishna. Balaram was one of the first patrons of Saradamani, and he arranged her relocation from Kamarpukur to Calcutta.

Bhairabi Brahmani (fl. 1860s): known also as Yogeshwari, Bhairabi appeared suddenly at Dakshineshwar and became Ramakrishna's tantric mentor. She was one of the first to declare the Master a divine incarnation. She accompanied him to Kamarpukur, where she reportedly imparted the tantric method of *sadhana*. She was noted for her mercurial temper and importuned young Sarada with her multiple demands. She disappeared in 1867 as mysteriously as she had arrived in Ramakrishna's life in 1861.

Brahmananda, Swami (1863–1922): monastic name of Rakhalchandra Ghosh, one of Ramakrishna's favorite disciples. Brahmananda was held in high esteem by Vivekananda (q.v.) and became the first president of the Ramakrishna Order in 1902 following Swamiji's death that year.

Datta, Ramchandra (1851–99): one of the most influential householder disciples of Ramakrishna and an elder cousin of Swami Vivekananda (q.v.). Datta was one of those devotees of the Master who had declared Ramakrishna's divinity, and he authored the latter's first full-blown biography, the *Ramakrishna Paramahamsadever Jibanbrittanta,* in 1890. He was also the first individual to build a temple for the regular worship of the Master's relics. It was built at his retreat, called Yogadyan, at Kankurgachhi in the northeastern suburb of Calcutta. Datta was somewhat cold toward Saradamani and did not treat her as generously as did other, less well-off devotees and disciples of Ramakrishna.

Gauri-ma (c. 1857–1938): popular appellation of Mridani Chattopadhyay of Shibpur, Howrah. Since childhood, Mridani had been a devotee of Kali. She went to an English middle school, where she did extremely well academically. However, she never wished to get married and hence left home and became a roving nun. She met the Master around 1882 and became his devotee and constant attendant. Later she became one of Saradamani's most intimate companions. She founded the Saradeshwari Ashrama at Barrackpore in 1894. She worked for the regeneration of Hindu women.

Ghatak, Lakshmimani (1864–1926): daughter of Ramakrishna's second elder brother, Rameshwar Chattopadhyay. Lakshmi, known by her affectionate name Lakshmi-didi, was married early to Dhanakrishna Ghatak of Goghat village. Her husband, however, mysteriously disappeared a couple of months after marriage, and Lakshmi performed the required rituals after waiting for him for twelve years, thus officially becoming a widow. She then came to live with her uncle Ramakrishna at Dakshineshwar and eventually became Saradamani's most intimate companion. Lakshmi was witty and fun-loving and was extremely popular among the Ramakrishna and Saradamani circles.

Ghosh, Girishchandra (1844–1912): an influential playwright, novelist, stage director, and actor in Calcutta. He was a householder disciple of Ramakrishna and proclaimed the divinity of Ramakrishna and Saradamani publicly.

Golap-ma (d. 1924): popular appellation of Golapsundari Devi, who was born in a poor Brahmin family of north Calcutta. (Her daughter, however, was to marry into one of the families of the Calcutta elite, the Tagores; her husband was the noted musician Saurendramohan Tagore.) Golap first met the Paramahamsa in 1885 and subsequently became Sarada's companion. Laura Glenn (Sister Devamata) described Golap as "tall and powerful in build, conservative, orthodox, and uncompromising"; she "acted as gendarme to Mother" but was altogether a kindhearted, simple, and loving soul. A devotee of Saradamani, Golap is reported to have said to her in Baranasi: "I do not want salvation. I want you."

Gopaler-ma (1822–1906): popular name of Aghormani Devi, who was initiated into Gopal mantras and hence was a devotee of Gopala, that is, the child Krishna. After she met Ramakrishna in 1884, she recognized him as the Srikrishna of

Dakshineshwar. She initiated a couple of devotees into *istamantra*. She was also an intimate elderly companion of the Holy Mother. Sister Nivedita (q.v.) was very devoted to her and took care of her meditation beads following her death.

Gupta, Mahendranath (or SriM) (1854–1932): served as headmaster in several Calcutta schools, and by the time he met Ramakrishna (February 1882), he had become headmaster of the Shyambazar branch of the Vidyasagar Institution. A householder disciple of the Master, SriM is the celebrated diarist who wrote the *Srisriramakrishnakathamrita* in five parts, published in 1902–32. He served the Holy Mother as sincerely and respectfully as he did Ramakrishna.

Mitra, Ashutosh (n.d.): premonastic name of Swami Satyakamananda, who was the younger brother of Swami Trigunatitananda (q.v.), a.k.a. Saradaprasanna Mitra, one of the direct disciples of Ramakrishna. Ashutosh kept a diary detailing his visits with Saradamani since 22 April 1898. It was published as *Srima* in 1944. Mitra's work was used as a source by Sarada's first biographer, Brahmachari Akshaychaitanya.

Mozoomdar, Protap Chunder (1840–1905): Brahmo scholar whose article on Ramakrishna in the *Theistic Quarterly Review* (October–December 1879) was one of the earliest to proclaim the purity of the *paramahamsa* among readers. He had been to the United States in 1883 as a lecturer on Vedanta as well as Brahmoism prior to his participation in the World Parliament of Religions in Chicago in 1893 as a member of the selection committee. It was Mozoomdar who accepted Vivekananda's late application without a letter of invitation and allowed him to participate in the parliament by classifying the swami as a representative of the Hindu monastic order. Mozoomdar criticized Ramakrishna's treatment of his wife as "barbarous" in a letter to Max Müller.

Mukhopadhyay, Hridayram (1840–99): Ramakrishna's cousin and his childhood companion and, after 1855, his factotum. Hriday eventually became a priest at the Dakshineshwar temple. He had a firsthand experience of Ramakrishna's ecstasy. He was habitually greedy and often fleeced many visitors desiring to visit with Ramakrishna. He was kicked out of his temple job after he was found performing *sodashi puja* on the eight-year-old granddaughter of Mathurmohan Biswas, manager and part owner of the Dakshineshwar temple.

Müller, Friedrich Max (1823–1900): the famous German Sanskrit and Vedic scholar of Oxford whom Vivekananda met in May 1896. Max Müller wrote a biographical article on Ramakrisha ("A Real Mahatman," *Nineteenth Century* 40 [1896]) and later *Ramakrishna: His Life and Sayings* (1898). He was critical of Vivekananda's interpretation of Ramakrishna's teachings as Vedantic.

Nag, Durgacharan (1846–99): a resident of Dhaka, Durgacharan became an admirer of Brahmoism at an early age. Following his encounter with Ramakrishna in 1882, he became an ardent, in fact a most perfervid, devotee of the Master as well as of the Holy Mother.

Nivedita, Sister (1867–1911): monastic name of Margaret Noble, a native of Ireland and a schoolteacher at Wimbledon, outside of London. Margaret met Vivekananda in London in 1895 and became his devotee and later, in Calcutta, his disciple. She was the spirit behind a girls' school at Baghbazar in northern Calcutta later named the Nivedita Girls' School. She was also an admirer and devotee of Saradamani. After Vivekananda's death in 1902, Nivedita left the Ramakrishna Order and devoted herself to the work of national and social regeneration in India, until her death at Darjeeling in 1911.

Premananda, Swami (1861–1918): monastic name of Baburam Ghosh, brother-in-law of Balaram Basu (q.v.), Ramakrishna's famous *zamindar* (landed gentry) disciple. He was an ardent follower of the *paramahamsa* as well as of the Holy Mother. He was somewhat skeptical of Vivekananda's (q.v.) interpretation of Ramakrishna's spiritual message, though eventually he reconciled himself to Swamiji's ways.

Ramakrishna Paramahamsa (1836–86): monastic name of Gadadhar Chattopadhyay, a semiliterate brahmin from the village of Kamarpukur and a priest of the temple of Bhavatarini (an appellation of the goddess Kali) at Dakshineshwar, founded by Rani Rasmani and managed by her son-in-law Mathurmohan Biswas. His spiritual message of "as many views so many venues" *(yata mat tata path)* and his ecstatic devotionalism were first propagandized by the Calcutta Brahmos and later spread in the West by his famous disciple Swami Vivekananda (q.v.).

Ramakrishnanada, Swami (1863–1911): monastic name of Shashibhusan Chakravarti and a disciple of Ramakrishna. At college, he had been attracted to the Brahmo Samaj movement and in fact came to hear of the Paramahamsa through the Brahmo press. He was a close associate of Vivekananda (q.v.) and solely responsible for the daily rituals at Baranagar Math. When the *math* shifted to Alambazar, his responsibilities increased. He later went to Madras (now Chennai) in 1897 at the behest of Vivekananda and organized the Ramakrishna Order in Madras and Bangalore.

Saradananda, Swami (1865–1927): monastic name of Sharatchandra Chakravarti, Ramakrishna's disciple. He visited England and the United States in 1896 to carry on Vivekananda's Vedantic mission there. He was appointed secretary to the Ramakrishna Mission by Swamiji. He was a deft organizer and the author of the magisterial biography of Ramakrishna, the *Srisriramakrishnalilaprasanga*. Saradananda was an assiduous manager of Saradamani's Calcutta home, which he had been instrumental in building.

Trigunatitananda, Swami (1865–1915): monastic name of Saradaprasanna Mitra, a disciple of Ramakrishna. He traveled to the United States in 1903 and worked with the Vedanta Society of California at San Francisco and Los Angeles until his death in 1915.

Virajananda, Swami (1873–1951): monastic name of Kalikrishna Basu, an admirer and a devotee of Vivekananda (q.v.) and Saradamani. He was drawn to the Ramakrishna Order following his acquaintance with SriM. He was initiated into *sannyasa* by Vivekananda. He became the general secretary of the Ramakrishna Math and Mission in 1934, and later its president.

Vivekananda, Swami (1863–1902): monastic name of Narendranath Datta of Calcutta, who had been a follower of the Brahmo Samaj in his early youth. He met Ramakrishna in 1881 and became his most beloved devotee and disciple. He earned renown abroad (United States and United Kingdom) as a Hindu preacher following his debut at the World's Parliament of Religions in Chicago in September 1893. He founded the Ramakrishna Order and declared Saradamani as the Mother of the Order *(sanghajanani)*. His celebrated Anglo-Irish disciple was Sister Nivedita (q.v.). His most popular appellation is Swamiji.

Yogananda, Swami (1861–99): monastic name of Yogindranath Ray Chaudhuri, devotee of Ramakrishna and his wife, Sarada. He hailed from the illustrious Chaudhuri family of Dakshineshwar. After Ramakrishna's death, Yogin became a caretaker of the Master's widow, Saradamani the Holy Mother and was initiated into *sannyasa* by her. Along with Premananda (q.v.), Yogananda once questioned Swamiji's refusal to regard the Master as an incarnation.

Yogen-ma (1851–1924): popular appellation of Yogindramohini Biswas née Mitra, daughter of the famous gynecologist of northern Calcutta Dr. Prasannakumar Mitra. Married in her early youth to the *zamindar* of Khardaha, Ambikacharan Biswas, Yogindramohini left her footloose and spendthrift spouse and went to live at the home of her kinsman and neighbor Balaram Basu in Baghbazar. She became a devotee of Balaram's guru, Sri Ramakrishna, sometime in 1883. Eventually she became attached to Saradamani as one of her most intimate companions. She tried her best to bring her wayward husband to the righteous path, but to no avail. Following Ambikacharan's and Ramakrishna's death, she became a constant companion to Sarada. She was initiated into *Kaulatantra* by Ishwar Chakravarti and into *sannyasa* by Swami Saradananda (q.v.). She died on 4 June 1924.

Notes

Preface

1. Sengupta, *Paramaprakriti Srisri Saradamani*, 235.

Chapter 1. Introduction

1. Müller, *Ramakrishna*, 65. Much of the information of this section is adapted from the excellent bibliographical essay by Sarkar, "Srima: Manisibrinder Dristite," 217–37. It must be borne in mind, however, that Max Müller had no access to the Bengali sources, and he relied heavily on some English essays on Ramakrishna by Protap Mozoomdar and Charles H. Tawney, and a biographical sketch by Swami Vivekananda.

2. Rolland, *Life of Ramakrishna*, 39–40.

3. Rüstau, "Ramakrishna Mission," 95, 102 n. 35.

4. *Prabuddha Bharata,* March 1954, 193–94, 126.

5. *Udbodhana* (Shatabarsa-Jayanti Sankhya), 1954, 46–50.

6. "Holy Mother–Ideal of Womanhood," 482.

7. Purnatmananda, *Chirantani Sarada*, 300.

8. Purnatmananda, "Sitarupini," 686.

9. For the attempt of some of these scholars to provide a theological/religious explanation—citing such scriptural texts as the *Rigveda, Shwetashwataropanisad, Kathopanisad, Srimadbhagavadgita, Srisrichandi, Vamakeshwaratantra,* Shankaracharya's *Anandalahari,* Kalidasa's *Raghuvamsam,* and the *Ramayana,* to name a select few—of Sarada's divinity, see Abjajananda, *Prakritim Paramam,* 1:1–157. See also Lokeshwarananda, *Shatarupe Sarada,* especially Jyotirmay Basuray, "Srima: Sriramakrishner Dashjan Shisyer Dristite" (78–111); Swami Hiranmayananda, "Swe Mahimni" (637–42); Gobindagopal Mukhopadhyay, "Shaktirupini" (643–51); Swami Purnatmananda, "Sitarupini" (652–86); Niradbaran Chakravarti, "Radharupini" (687–95); and Belarani De, "Swayambadini" (696–708). See also Prabhananda, *Srisirsaradamahima.* The only academic treatment of Sarada's holy motherhood—not entirely convincing, though, in many ways, a valiant effort—remains McDaniel, *Madness of Saints*, 202–9.

10. Akshaychaitanya, *Swami Saradanander Patramala*, 101. I thank Rajagopal Chattopadhyaya for having drawn my attention to this collection.

11. Dimock, "Religious Biography," 109.

12. Reynolds and Capps, *Biographical Process*, 3 cited in Hallstrom, *Mother of Bliss*, 22.

13. Rinehart, *One Lifetime, Many Lives*, 3.

14. Khandelwal, "Ungendered *Atma*," 99.

15. Kripal, "Perfecting the Mother's Silence."

16. Mukharji, "Sarada Devi," 137.

17. Mukherjee, "Nabajagaran, Samaj-Bibartan O Saradadevi," 427.

18. Gupta, "Goddess, Women, and Their Rituals in Hinduism," 92.

19. Cited in Bhattacharya, "Bharatiya Chintadharay Shaktitatwa O Srima," 577.

20. Wadley, "Woman and Hindu Tradition," 117–18. See also Smith, "Indra's Curse, Varuna's Noose, and Suppression of Woman," 17–45. See also Samanta, *Mangalmayima Simangali, Mangal.*

21. Gupta, "Goddess, Women, and Their Rituals in Hinduism," 95.

22. Jacobson, "Female Pole in Tantrism and Samkhya," 59.

23. The historical and sociocultural reasons for this failure need not detain us here. Suffice it to say that the rise of the goddess in Hinduism was synchronous with the matriarchal societies of ancient India. However, as Narendranath Bhattacharyya has observed, "under diverse historical conditions Tantrism eventually came under the very masculine Vedantic fold." *History of the Tantric Religion*, ix.

24. Vivekananda, *Patrabali*, 99: Vivekananda's letter of 28 December 1893 from the United States.

25. McKibbin, "Personalities of Prakriti," 271.

26. Wadley, "Paradoxical Powers of Tamil Women."

27. Apte, "Social and Economic Condition in Epic Times," 391.

28. Pandey, "Hindu View on Women," 43.

29. Hughes, *Epic Women East and West*, 36.

30. Ibid., 42.

31. Ibid., 78–79. See also Dumézil, *Mythe et Épopée*. For Madhavi's story see Basu, *Krishnadwaipayaya Byaskrita Mahabharata.*

32. What follows is drawn freely from Chatterjee, "Nationalist Resolution of the Women's Question," 233–53.

33. See Kopf, "Brahmo Idea of Social Reform," 35–58.

34. Chatterjee, "Nationalist Resolution of the Women's Question," 249. Himani Bannerji rightly questions the current political manipulation of this idealized womanhood ("Pygmalion womanhood"), but Chatterjee is right on the mark in detecting its development in the nineteenth century. See Bannerji, "Pygmalion Nation," 34–84.

35. Bagchi, "Representing Nationalism," WS 71.

36. Sarkar, "Nationalist Iconography," WS 2011–51.

37. Bagchi, "Representing Nationalism," WS 70.

38. Auerbach, *Woman and Demon*, 219, cited in Bhattacharji, "Motherhood in Ancient India," WS 54.

39. Walsh, "Virtuous Wife and the Well-Ordered Home," 357.

40. Forbes, "Ideals of Indian Womanhood," 71.

Chapter 2. Saradamani's Early Life

1. Dasgupta, *Saradadevi: Atmakatha*, 3.

2. Ibid., 8.

3. Ibid., 4.

4. Ghanananda, "Sri Sarada Devi the Holy Mother," 95.

5. Gambhirananda, *Holy Mother Sri Sarada Devi*, 21.
6. Bhumananda, *Srisri Mayer Jiban-katha*, 13.
7. Ibid.,10.
8. Aksaychaitanya, *Thakur Sriramakrishna*, 130.
9. Ibid.,13.
10. Gambhirananda, *Holy Mother Sri Sarada Devi*, 114–15.
11. Akshaychaitanya, *Srisrisaradadevi*, 52n.
12. Gaurishwarananda, "Ma Ke Yeman Dekhechhi," 259.
13. Gambhirananda, *Holy Mother Sri Sarada Devi*, 173.
14. Saradananda, *Srisriramakrishnalilaprasanga*, 2:268 (Thakurer Divyabhava O Narendranath).

CHAPTER 3. SARADAMANI'S HUSBAND, THE MARRIED CELEBATE

This chapter is derived principally from my *Ramakrishna Revisited*, chap. 4
1. Nirvedananda, "Ramakrishna and Spiritual Renaissance," 2:507.
2. Gupta (SriM), *Srisriramakrishnakathamrita*, 2:49 (diary of 4 June 1883).
3. Cited in Devi, *Sarada-Ramakrishna*, 52.
4. Saradananda, *Srisriramakrishnalilaprasanga*, 1:128–44 (Gurubhava-Purvardha).
5. Kripal, *Kali's Child*, 117–30.
6. Datta, *Srisriramakrishna Paramahamsadever Jibanbrittanta*, 33.
7. Saradananda, *Srisriramakrishnalilaprasanga*, 1:202 (Sadhakabhava).
8. Barman, *Srisriramakrishnacharit*, 1:69.
9. Datta, *Srisriramakrishna Paramahamsadever Jibanbrittanta*, 31.
10. Ibid., 37.
11. Ibid., 33–34.
12. Ibid., 34.
13. Chetanananda, *Matridarshan*, 273: conversation of Swami Saradananda (Sharatchandra Chakravarti) with Mrinalini Devi.
14. Gambhirananda, *Holy Mother Sri Sarada Devi*, 36.
15. Saradananda, *Srisriramakrishnalilaprasanga,* 1:352 (Sadhakabhava).
16. Matilal, *Sriramakrishner Dampatyajiban*, 3.
17. Devi, *Sarada-Ramakrishna*, 29.
18. Bharatiprana, "Reminiscences of Holy Mother and Nivedita," 150, cited in Robinson, "Ramakrishna Sarada Math," 182.
19. Gambhirananda, *Holy Mother Sri Sarada Devi*, 114.
20. See note 70 below.
21. See Meissner, *Psychology of a Saint,* chap. 19: "Mysticism: Psychoanalytic View."
22. For a detailed analysis of this issue, see Sil, *Ramakrishna Revisited*, chap. 3: "Ramakrishna's Androgyny."
23. Saradananda, *Srisriramakrishnalilaprasanga*, 1:92 (Purvakatha O Valyajivana and Sadhakabhava).
24. According to popular beliefs, the child Gadadhar experienced samadhi for the first time at the age of six when he beheld white cranes flying in the sky overcast with dark clouds. For an explanation of this condition, see Sil, *Ramakrishna Revisited,* 139–52.
25. Saradananda, *Srisriramakrishnalilaprasanga*, 1:276 (Sadhakabhava).
26. Saradananda, *Srisriramakrishnalilaprasanga*, 1:193 (Gurubhava-Purvardha).
27. Datta, *Sriramakrishner Anudhyan*, 149. For more information on gynecomastia, see the website wysiwyg://24/http://abcnews.go.com.../2020/2020_010323_malebreasts. html.

28. Gupta (SriM), *Srisriramakrishnakathamrita*, 4:259 (diary of 23 October 1885).

29. Ibid., 2:207 (diary of 24 April 1885).

30. Sanyal, *Sriramakrishna Lilamrita*, 159.

31. See Pauly, "Adult Manifestations of Male Transsexualism," 37–58. Ramakrishna could also be described as a "she male," that is, a male who, despite his male genitalia, possesses a female psyche and breasts resembling those of a woman. See the feature on *The Sally Jesse Raphael Show* entitled "She Male" that aired on CBS (28 August 1989).

32. Saradananda, *Srisriramakrishnalilaprasanga*, 1:269, 272 (Sadhakabhava).

33. Ibid., 274. Anthropologists and psychohistorians report on male simulation of menstruation among several primitive cultures. Even as late as the seventh century the Byzantine writer Paul of Aegina (625–90) mentioned about "hemorrhoidal flux" or "hemorrhoidal bleeding" as the male counterpart to female menstruation. See Brain, "Male Menstruation," 316.

34. Money, *Venuses Penuses*, 454.

35. Ibid., 466–68.

36. Gupta (SriM), *Srisriramakrishnakathamrita*, 4:201 (diary of 5 October 1884).

37. Erikson, *Identity,* 179. See also 167–69.

38. Sil, *Ramakrishna Revisited*, 35ff.

39. Laing, *Divided Self,* 44. See also Dewart, "Writings of Laing."

40. Gupta (SriM), *Srisriramakrishnakathamrita*, 4:4 (diary of 1 January 1883).

41. Ibid., 4:74 (diary of 24 February 1884).

42. Ibid., 2:231 (diary of 22 April 1886).

43. Erikson, *Identity,* 186.

44. See Haberman, *Acting as a Way to Salvation*, 94–108.

45. Gupta (SriM), *Srisriramakrishnakathamrita*, 3:22 (diary of 24 August 1882).

46. Ibid., 5:51 (diary of 10 June 1883. The Vaishnavic conception of *kama* (eros) and *prema* (celestial love, somewhat analogous to the Christian *agape*) is popularized in Krishnadas Kabiraj's *Chaitanyacharitamrita:* "atmendriya pritibanchha tare bali kam. Krishnendriya pritibanchha dhare premnam" [desires centered on the self are lust (carnal love), but those centered on Krishna are love proper, that is, *prema*]. See Adilila, 4:139.

47. Ibid., 4:36 (diary of 17 December 1883).

48. Kakar, *Shamans, Mystics, and Doctors*, 156.

49. Sen, *Ramakrishnapunthi*, 74–75.

50. Saradananda, *Srisriramakrishnalilaprasanga*, 1:168 (Sadhakabhava).

51. Datta, *Srisriramakrishna Paramahamsadever Jibanbrittanta*, 36. Bengali prostitutes in the nineteenth century used to suck the toe of their aging male customers (presumably incapable of achieving erections) by way of humbling and debasing themselves before pleading for a favor or a gift. Gangopadhyay, *Sei Samay*, 141.

52. Gambhirananda, *Holy Mother Sri Sarada Devi*, 127.

53. Dasgupta, *Saradadevi: Atmakatha*, 42.

54. Basu, *Bhagaban Sriramakrishnadeber Balyalila*, 34.

55. Carstairs, "Hinjra and Jiryan," 134.

56. Gatwood, *Devi and the Spouse Goddess*, 177.

57. Chatterjee, "Religion of Urban Domesticity," 60.

58. Ghosal, *Mukti ebam Tahar Sadhan*, 116–29. This is the unabridged edition of the original preserved in the library of the Belur Math.

59. Gupta (SriM), *Srisriramakrishnakathamrita*, 4:89 (diary of 23 March 1884).

60. Spratt, *Hindu Culture and Personality*, 92; Carstairs, "Hinjra and Jiryan," 133.

61. Cited in Rudolph, *Modernity of Tradition*, 196.

62. Bharati, "Hindu Renaissance," 285.

63. Masson, "Psychology of the Ascetic," 617.

64. Saradananda, *Srisriramakrishnalilaprasanga*, 1:217 (Gurubhava-Purvardha).

65. Matilal, *Sriramakrishner Dampatyajiban,* 108. Reportedly, this incident was re-lated by Saradamani herself.

66. Cited in Mookerjee, *Sriramakrishna in the Eyes of Brahmo and Christian Admir-ers,* 14.

67. Gupta (SriM), *Srisriramakrishnakathamrita,* 4:201 (diary of 5 October 1884).

68. Ibid., 4:164 (diary of 19 September 1884); 2:154 (diary of 11 October 1884). The Vaishnava sect of Ghoshopara Village is called Kartabhaja.

69. Saradananda, *Srisriramakrishnalilaprasanga,* 2:163 (Thakurer Divyabhava O Narendranath).

70. Mitra, *Sriramakrishna (Jibani O Upadesh),* 34–35.

71. Gupta (SriM), *Srisriramakrishnakathamrita,* 3:19 (diary of 24 August 1882),

72. Ibid., 2:11 (diary of 17 October 1882).

73. Jagadishwarananda, *Sriramakrishnaparsadprasanga,* 191–92.

74. Nirlepananda, *Ramakrishna Saradamrita,* 10: Lakshmimani's deposition (15 June 1925). I thank Rajagopal Chattopadhyaya for suggesting this work.

75. Dasgupta, *Saradadevi: Atmakatha,* 68–69. Evidently Ramakrishna was quite sus-picious even of his own devotees!

76. Nirlepananda, *Ramakrishna Saradamrita,* 4.

77. Bhattacharya, *SriMar Jibandarshan,* 81.

78. Datta, *Sriramakrishnadever Upadesh,* 142 (# 508).

79. Gupta (SriM), *Srisriramakrishnakathamrita,* 4:83 (diary of 23 March 1884); 5:55 (diary of 17 June 1883).

80. McLean, "Women as Aspects of Mother Goddess in India," 15.

81. Ibid.

CHAPTER 4. SARADAMANI AS *PARAMAHAMSA*'S WIFE

This chapter is based partly on my *Ramakrishna Revisited,* chap. 9.

1. Saradananda, *Srisriramakrishnalilaprasanga,* 1:362 (Sadhakabhava); Gupta (SriM), *Srisriramakrishnakathamrita,* 2:155 (diary of 11 October 1884).

2. Ibid., 1:242 (Gurubhava-Purvardha); Gambhirananda, *Holy Mother Sri Sarada Devi,* 36–37; Her Devotee-Children, *Gospel of the Holy Mother,* 215.

3. Gambhirananda, *Holy Mother Sri Sarada Devi,* 40.

4. Ibid., 114–15. The word *sarada* means the bestower of *sara,* that is, knowledge.

5. Arupananda, "Sriramakrishner 'Shakti'," 2.

6. Nikhilananda, *Holy Mother,* 65.

7. *Life of Sri Ramakrishna Compiled from Various Sources,* 252.

8. Nivedita, *Letters of Nivedita,* 2:717: Nivedita's letter of 4 February 1905 to Miss MacLeod (emphasis in original). However, this could be interpreted as Ramakrishna imply-ing that Sarada had gone beyond the level of a *jivanmukta* or a liberated soul, because he had accorded her the higher status of a goddess.

9. Nikhilananda, *Holy Mother,* 46.

10. Gambhirananda, *Holy Mother Sri Sarada Devi,* 49–50. Ramakrishna may have imitated his friend the tantric pandit Gaurikanta Tarkabhusan, who reportedly worshiped his wife with flowers, believing her to be the goddess Bhagavati in human form. Gupta (SriM), *Srisriramakrishnakathamrita,* 4:74 (diary of 24 February 1884).

11. Gupta (SriM), *Srisriramakrishnakathamrita,* 4:74 (diary of 24 February 1884).

12. Gambhirananda, *Holy Mother Sri Sarada Devi,* 49.

13. Ibid., 50.

14. Brown, *Wieland,* 196–97.

15. It should be noted that she could not live with her husband at Dakshineshwar permanently. She went back to Kamarpukur in October 1873 and returned to Dakshineshwar the following April. She left for Jairambati in September 1875 following an attack of dysentery. She paid a brief visit to Dakshineshwar in March 1876, returning to her village sometime during late 1876 or early 1877. She was back to Dakshineshwar in February 1878 and again left for her ancestral home following her ill treatment at the hands of her husband's nephew Hridayram. After Hriday's ouster from employment at the Kali temple in 1881, she returned to Daķshineshwar in March 1882 to look after her husband in the absence of a boon companion and a factotum. She visited her village in 1883 and lived there for seven to eight months, returning to Dakshineshwar in late 1883. Unfortunately, her visit this time was considered inauspicious by her husband, as he broke his arm in an accident; and she was commanded by him to go back immediately and restart her journey to Dakshineshwar from Jairambati. This she did and returned to her husband within a few days. In 1884 she traveled to Kamarpukur to attend the marriage of Ramalal, another nephew of Ramakrishna, and came back to her husband in March 1885. She was present at his death in 1886. Gambhirananda, *Holy Mother Sri Sarada Devi,* 42–53.

16. Nikhilananda, *Holy Mother,* 47.

17. Gambhirananda, *Holy Mother Sri Sarada Devi,* 60–61. Later Sarada would claim the Jagaddhatri identity for herself.

18. Nikhilananda, *Holy Mother,* 51.

19. Devi, *Sarada-Ramakrishna,* 125.

20. Nirvedananda, "Sriramakrishna and Spiritual Renaissance," 507.

21. Apurbananda, *Sriramakrishna O Srima,* 185.

22. Saradananda, *Srisriramakrishnalilaprasanga,* 1:133 (Gurubhava-Purvardha).

23. Ibid., 1:156 (Sadhakabhava).

24. Nikhilananda, *Holy Mother,* 31.

25. Ibid.

26. Ibid., 65.

27. Gupta (SriM), *Srisriramakrishnakathamrita,* 4:28–29 (diary of 15 December 1883): Ramakrishna's admonition to SriM.

28. *Life of Ramakrishna Compiled from Various Sources,* 488.

29. Gupta (SriM), *Srisriramakrishnakathamrita,* 3:100 (diary of 9 November 1884).

30. Saradananda, *Srisriramakrishnalilaprasanga,* 1:35 (Gurubhava-Purvardha).

31. Arupananda, *Srisrimayer Katha,* 214–15.

32. Gupta (SriM), *Srisriramakrishnakathamrita,* 1:188 (diary of 11 March 1885).

33. Akhandananda, *Smriti-katha,* 9.

34. Gupta (SriM), *Srisriramakrishnakathamrita,* 1:189 (diary of 11 March 1885); 3:102, 260 (diaries of 9 November 1884, 13 April 1886); 4:249 (31 August 1885).

35. Ibid., 2:131 (diary of 26 September 1884); *Bhagavat Gita,* trans. Prabhavananda and Isherwood, 45, 78.

36. Gupta (SriM), *Srisriramakrishnakathamrita,* 3:178 (diary of 13 June 1885).

37. Gambhirananda, *Holy Mother Sri Sarada Devi,* 76–77.

38. Gupta (SriM), *Srisriramakrishnakathamrita,* 14–15 (diary of 26 February 1882).

39. Ibid., 5:72 (diary of 22 February 1885).

40. Ibid., 3:76 (diary of 30 June 1884).

41. Nikhilananda, *Holy Mother,* 58.

42. Ibid., 55–56.

43. Nikhilananda, *Sri Sarada Devi the Holy Mother (Conversations),* 65n.

44. Nikhilananda, *Holy Mother,* 56.

45. Gambhirananda, *Holy Mother Sri Sarada Devi,* 123.

46. Ibid., 76.

47. Tapasyananda, *Sri Sarada Devi the Holy Mother*, 30.

48. Gambhirananda, *Holy Mother Sri Sarada Devi*, 111.

49. See note 6 above.

50. Prabhananda, *First Meetings with Sri Ramakrishna*, 143.

51. Gambhirananda, *Holy Mother Sri Sarada Devi*, 66.

52. Mitra, *Srisriramakrishna Paramahamsa*, 152. The Bengali word *shala* used by the Master literally means "wife's brother" but may also be used as a term of abuse that makes the user the victim's "sister fucker." Ramakrishna used it as a general form of abuse for castigating the bratty Brahmo, and I translate it as the popular expression of abuse in American English, "son of a bitch," to highlight the anger of Ramakrishna's retort.

53. Bhumananda, *Srisrimayer Jiban-katha*, 102.

54. Ibid., 79.

55. Ibid., 104.

56. Ibid., 98–104.

57. Sil, *Swami Vivekananda*, chap. 3.

58. Bhumananda, *Srisrimayer Jiban-katha*, 104.

59. Devi, *Sarada-Ramakrishna*, 169. For a succinct account of Sarada's problem of where to stay after her husband's death in 1886 see Tapasyananda, *Sarada Devi*, 37–47. She finally came down to Calcutta and lived there until her death in 1920.

60. Bhumananda, *Srisrimayer Jiban-katha*, 104.

61. Gambhirananda, *Holy Mother Sri Sarada Devi*, 164.

62. Bhumananda, *Srisrimayer Jiban-katha*, 107.

63. Gambhirananda, *Holy Mother Sri Sarada Devi*, 168.

64. Ibid., 213.

65. Ibid., 175–76.

66. Gambhirananda, *Holy Mother Sri Sarada Devi*, 215–16.

67. Ibid., 217–18.

68. Ibid., 219–20.

69. Cited in Hiranmayananda, "Swe Mahimni," 639.

70. Sil, *Swami Vivekananda*, chap. 8; idem, *Ramakrishna Revisited*, chap. 9.

71. Vivekananda, *Complete Works*, 8:80–82: Vivekananda's lecture "My Life and Mission" delivered at the Shakespeare Club of Pasadena (27 January 1900).

72. Vivekananda, *Patrabali*, 257: letter of 1894.

73. Vivekananda, *Complete Works*, vol. 7, letter #23: Vivekananda's letter to Manmathanath Bhattacharya (5 September 1894). This letter, written originally in Bengali, is partially reprinted in *Patrabali*.

74. Cited in Prabhananda, "Vivekananda and His 'Only Mother'," 18. Bagala is one of the goddesses of the tantric pantheon and one of the ten manifestations of Kali the Great Mother.

75. Ibid., 10.

76. Vivekananda, *Patrabali*, 256: Vivekananda's letter (1894).

77. Dhar, *Comprehensive Biography*, 2:947.

78. Vivekananda, *Patrabali*, 449: Vivekananda's letter (April 1896).

79. Ibid., 421: Vivekananda's letter (1895).

80. See Sil, *Ramakrishna Revisited*, chap. 10.

CHAPTER 5. SARADAMANI'S DIVINE MOTHERHOOD

1. Gambhirananda, *Holy Mother Sri Sarada Devi*, 465; Her Devotee-Children, *Gospel of the Holy Mother*, 303; Nikhilananda, *Holy Mother*, 187.

2. Archanapuri, *Saradeshwari*, 172.

3. Mitra, "Srima," 2:346.

4. Arupananda, *Srisrimayer Katha*, 98.

5. Ray, "Ma ke Pratham Dekhi," 1:86.

6. Chetanananda, *Matridarshan*, 218–19.

7. Saradeshananda, *Srisrimayer Smritikatha*, 125.

8. Akshaychaitanya, *Saradadevi*, 108.

9. Ibid., 117.

10. Ibid., 140. Sen's *Punthi*, published in 1901, was a biography of Ramakrishna in verse.

11. Akshaychaitanya, *Srisrisaradadevi*, 140n.

12. Ibid.

13. Nag, "Kemane Bhuli Karuna Tanr," 1:94–95.

14. Nirvanananda, "Matrisannidhye," 1:27.

15. Personal interview with Surendra's son Ranendranath Banerjee and his wife, Rina (Calcutta, 17 September 1997). I thank Ranjana Mukherjee for introducing me to the Banerjees.

16. Cited in Hiranmayananda, "Holy Mother Ideal," 110.

17. Mitra, "Srima," 2:343.

18. Cited in "Bibidh" [Miscellaneous] in Lokeshwarananda, *Shatarupe Sarada*, 783–84.

19. Chetanananda, *Matridarshan*, 176–77.

20. Purnatmananda, *Srisrimayer Padaprante*, 3:610.

21. Ishanananda, *Matrisanniddhye*, 9–10.

22. The quotes from Vivekananda and Ram Datta are cited in Sil, "Vivekananda's Concept of Woman," 40–41.

23. Abjajananda, *Prakritim Paramam*, 1:1,2,5; Arupananda, *Srisrimayer Katha*, 170n.

24. Purnatmananda, *Srisrimayer Padaprante*, 3:509.

25. Cited in Mitra, "Srima," 2:320. See 321–22 for Padmavinod's terminal illness. It is to be noted that Padmabinod's stage colleague Girish used to visit the *parasmahamsa* at Dakshineshwar in the dead of night after having had a drinking spree with his buddies in the early evening.

26. Devi, *Sarada-Ramakrishna*, 211–13.

27. Ibid., 319–20.

28. Abjajananda, *Prakritim Paramam*, 1, 2, 5 (see 1–157 for a detailed canonical explanation of Sarada's Kali identity.

29. Satswarupananda, "Karunamayi," 1:63.

30. Ishanananda, *Matrisanniddhye*, 131.

31. Gambhirananda, *Holy Mother Sri Sarada Devi*, 156–57. This seems to be a garbled account of the young man's attempted rape. Reportedly a boy of character and devotion, he lost his head after marriage when his in-laws forced him to consume some sort of magical aphrodisiac with a view to turning his mind from asceticism to his wife. He attacked Sarada in such a state of mind. The utterly improbable story of the widow's defending herself by assuming her *swarupa* as the Goddess Bagala was started by Sarada herself and further colored by her devotees and hagiographers and it was designed to highlight her divinity. Realistically speaking, Sarada could not possibly have pulled the young man's tongue in the manner of the goddess as is familiar in folk painting of the ten Mahavidyas, though it is reasonable to suppose that somehow she might have overpowered him and protected herself from becoming a victim of rape. Jeffrey Kripal cites Arupananda, *Srisrimayer Katha* (174) and Her Devotee-Children, *Gospel of the Holy Mother* (78n) and makes Harish her "crazed cousin" (Harish's surname Mustafi is confused with Mukhopadhyay which is Sarada's maiden

surname) by whom she was "chased around the village" (the incident occurred in the compound of her home). This is a case of strange invention to illustrate "Sharada's" [*sic*] silence. Kripal's explanation of Sarada's deification follows his favorite interpretation of Hindu spirituality and mysticism in terms of something dark and mysterious: hidden, forbidden, secret, and silent. Kripal, "Perfecting the Mother's Silence," 187.

32. Archanapuri, *Saradeshwari*, 172–73.

33. Mitra, "Srima," 2:294.

34. Cited in Basu, "Niveditar Dhruvamandir," 157.

35. Akshaychaitanya, *Srisaradadevi*, 114n.

36. Her Devotee-Children, *Gospel of the Holy Mother*, 303. Koalpara, a village near Jairambati, is the site of two establishments of the Ramakrishna Order: Koalpara Ashrama for men and Jagadamba Ashrama for Sarada's temporary resting place on her way to Jairambati. Both were built, most probably, by her devotee Kedarnath Datta, a local worthy.

37. Nikhilananda, *Holy Mother*, 187. See also Akshaychaitanya, *Srisaradadevi*, 114; Purnatmananda, *Srisrimayer Padaprante*, 3:615.

38. Purnatmananda, *Srisrimayer Padaprante*, 3;629.

39. Datta, "Punyasmriti," 1:123.

40. Purnatmananda, *Srisrimayer Padaprante*, 3:654.

41. Ibid., 571.

42. Her Devotee-Children, *Gospel of the Holy Mother*, 301.

43. Gambhirananda, *Holy Mother Sri Sarada Devi*, 465.

44. See below, chap. 7, n. 11.

45. Dasgupta, *Saradadevi: Atmakatha*, 79.

46. See chap. 4, n. 51 above.

47. Ishanananda, *Matrisanniddhye*, 165–66.

48. Gambhirananda, *Holy Mother Sri Sarada Devi*, 381–82.

49. Ishanananda, *Matrisanniddhye*, 166.

50. Her Devotee-Children, *Gospel of the Holy Mother*, 343: reminiscences of Swami Maheswarananda.

51. Akshaychaitanya, *Srisaradadevi*, 111–12.

52. Chetanananda, *Matridarshan*, 157-58.

53. Personal communication from Dr. McDermott (letter of 31 January 1997).

54. See Gupta, "Kali the Savior." Bengalis adore Kali the mother figure rather than Kali the liberator of women. See McDermott's doctoral dissertation "Evidence for Transformation of the Goddess Kali" and her *Mother of My Heart, Daughter of My Dreams*.

55. Purnatmananda, *Chirantani Sarada*, 2–6.

56. Her Devotee-Children, *Gospel of the Holy Mother*, xxxix.

57. Swami Prabhananda has written a lengthy article on Swamiji's claim. See "Vivekananda and His 'Only Mother'."

58. Tagore, *Tagore Testament*, 20.

CHAPTER 6. SARADAMANI'S MATERNAL TRIUMPH

1. Devi, *Sarada-Ramakrishna*, 98.

2. Purnatmananda, *Srisrimayer Padaprante*, 2;433 [unpublished diary of SriM].

3. Gambhirananda, *Holy Mother Sri Sarada Devi*, 126–27.

4. Prabhananda, "Vivekananda and His 'Only Mother'," 12.

5. Akshayahaitanya, *Srisrisaradadevi*, 77 (see also 78–106).

6. Chetanananda, *Matridarshan*, 6–7.

7. Ibid., 10. The English words in quotes are Birajananda's own.

8. Purnatmananda, *Srisrimayer Padaprante*, 3;571.

9. Ibid., 624.

10. Chetanananda, *Matridarshan*, 16.

11. Ibid., 23.

12. Ibid., 231.

13. Saradeshananda, "Matrisamipe," 1:5.

14. Ibid., 7.

15. Ibid., 38–39.

16. Akshaychaitanya, *Srisaradadevi*, 98: reminiscences of Rakhal Nag.

17. Chetanananda, *Matridarshan*, 171: reminiscences of Srigokul.

18. Purnatmananda, *Srisrimayer Padaprante*, 1:24–25.

19. Chetanananda, *Matridarshan*, 273.

20. Canetti, *Crowds and Power*, 221, cited in Bynum, *Holy Feast and Holy Fast*, 190.

21. Ibid., 191.

22. See chap. 4, n. 21, above.

23. Among nearly eleven hundred initiated disciples of the Holy Mother, there were about 180 who became monks. See Purnatmananda, *Srisrimayer Padaprante*, 2;442–79.

CHAPTER 7. SARADA'S FORMATIVE YEARS

1. Bhumananda, *Srisrimayer Jiban-katha*, 113. The iconic masklike face of the image of Jagannath does resemble that of the stylized lion in the art of Orissa.

2. Ibid., 118.

3. Ibid., 126. See also chap. 4, n. 65, above. Nag was noted for his wacky behavior. Once, reprimanded by his father for having abandoned his medical practice and warned by him that he would "go naked and live on frogs," the young Durgacharan "immediately stripped himself, picked up a dead frog from the courtyard and started eating it." He then told his father: "Please don't worry about my food and clothing any longer." Chetanananda, *They Lived with God*, 216.

4. Purnatmananda, *Srisrimayer Padaprante*, 2:435.

5. Her Devotee-Children, *Gospel of the Holy Mother*, 185.

6. Bhumananda, *Srisri Mayer Jiban-katha*, 137.

7. Ibid., 142–43.

8. Nivedita, *Letters of Nivedita,* 2:631.

9. Nikhilananda, *Holy Mother*, 304. According to Swami Ishanananda, Sarada's comment was made during her conversations at her Calcutta home, Udbodhana, with Swami Keshavananda of Koalpara Ashrama sometime in August 1912. Chetanananda, *Matridarshan*, 18.

10. Ibid., 307.

11. Arupananda, *Srisrimayer Katha*, 233.

12. Nikhilananda, *Holy Mother,* 309.

13. Ibid., 310.

14. Ibid., 311.

15. Ibid., 315–16.

16. Ibid., 318.

17. Bharatiprana, "Srisrimayer Charanaprante," 3:518. For a most vivid account of Sarada's last days, see 510–21.

18. Ibid., 520.

19. Devi, *Sarada-Ramakrishna*, 432.

CHAPTER 8. SARADA

1. Muktiprana, *Srima Sarada*, 35.
2. Arupananda, *Srisrimayer Katha*, 295: reminiscences of Swami Vireshwarananda. For Sarada's ordeal with Radhu (Radharani), Ramakrishna's mentally disturbed niece, see the chapter titled "Radhu" in Gambhirananda, *Holy Mother Sri Sarada Devi*.
3. Chetanananda, *Matridarshan,* 158.
4. Sarada's letter of 15 Bhadra 1309 B.E., cited in Basu, "Niveditar Dhruvamandir," 165.
5. Chetanananda, *Matridarshan,* 159.
6. Ibid., 214–15: reminiscences of Amulyabandhu Mukhopadhyay.
7. Gambhirananda, *Holy Mother Sri Sarada Devi,* 370.
8. Saradeshananda, *Srisrimayer Smritikatha,* 50.
9. Bhumananda, *Srisrimayer Jiban-katha,* 228.
10. Chetanananda, *Matridarshan,* 75.
11. Ishanananda, *Matrisanniddhye,* 49.
12. Ibid., 64.
13. Chetanananda, *Matridarshan,* 55.
14. Nikhilananda, *Holy Mother,* 302.
15. Ibid., 52. Sarada gave the following reason for not accepting the initiate's sins: "Kashite ya kara yay, ta aksay hai. Diksa diye ami shisyer pap grahan kari. Papke aksay kare neba kena?" [Whatever is done in Kashi {Benares} remains for ever. I accept the disciple's sins when I initiate him. Why should I bear the sins forever?]. The popular belief, of course, was that all sins are washed off in Benares.
16. Personal interview with Ranendranath and Rina Banerjee.
17. Bhumananda, *Srisri Mayer Jiban-katha,* 230.
18. Mitra, "Srima," 2:339.
19. Cited in Mukhopadhyay, "Bharater Swadhinata-Sangram," 449.
20. Her Devotee-Children, *Gospel of the Holy Mother,* 273, 291.
21. Chetanananda, *Matridarshan,* 273.
22. Nikhilananda, *Sri Sarada Devi the Holy Mother (Conversations),* 359.
23. Devi, *Sarada-Ramakrishna,* 129.
24. Arupananda, *Srisrimayer Katha,* 104. Kripal's translation "that Ma had sent me [Surendra] to M [Gupta] to make me understand the meaning of her glance of grace" is an instance of his famous innovation. Kripal, "Perfecting the Mother's Silence," 188. The original Bengali has it: "Tanhar padadhuli laiya Sriyukta Master Mahashayer badi Guruprasad Chaudhuri Laney upasthit hailam" [Having having saluted her by touching her feet I arrived at the home of Sriyukta Master Mahashay in Guruprasad Chaudhuri Lane]. Arupananda, *Srisrimayer Katha,* 104.
25. Mumukshananda, "Srisrima," 596, 608.
26. Gambhirananda, *Holy Mother Sri Sarada Devi,* 4.
27. Ibid., 6.
28. Cited in Bharadwaj, "Saradadevi ebam Adhunikata," 526.
29. See nn. 6 and 7 above.
30. Bharadwaj, "Saradadevi ebam Adhunikata," 527.
31. Cited in ibid., 534.
32. Ibid., 529.
33. Ibid., 534.
34. Gambhirananda, *Holy Mother Sri Sarada Devi,* 264.
35. Bharadwaj, "Saradadevi ebam Adhunikata," 529.

36. Gambhirananda, *Holy Mother Sri Sarada Devi*, 390.

37. Someshwarananda, "Saradadevir Yuktinistha O Samajchetana," 477.

38. Ibid., 533.

39. Gambhirananda, *Holy Mother Sri Sarada Devi*, 372.

40. Bhumananda, *Srisrimayer Jiban-katha*, 231.

41. Das, "Pisimar Katha," 677.

42. Denton, "Varieties of Hindu Female Asceticism," 212–14. See also McDaniel, *Madness of Saints*, 230–31.

43. Arupananda, *Srisrimayer Katha*, 154–55.

44. Ibid., 47 (recorded by Sarayubala Devi).

45. Gupta, "Women in the Shaiva/Shakta Ethos," 194.

46. See Ojha, "Feminine Asceticism in Hinduism," 254–85. See also Denton, "Varieties of Hindu Female Asceticism," 211–50.

47. Budhananda, *Sriramakrishna-Bibhasita Ma Sarada*, 64ff.

48. Ibid., 70.

49. Gambhirananda, *Holy Mother Sri Sarada Devi*, 1, citing Saradananda, *Bharate Shaki Puja*, 20.

50. Ibid.

51. See Leslie's introduction to *Roles and Rituals for Hindu Women;* and idem, "Ambivalent Role Models for Women," 107–27.

52. See Sarkar, "'Kaliyuga,' 'Chakri', and 'Bhakti'"; and Chatterjee, "A Religion of Urban Domesticity," 40–68.

53. Ghosh, "Sahadharmini," 336.

54. Bandyopadhyay, "Banglar Lokasamskritir Dhara O Srima Sarada," 549.

55. See chap. 4, n. 54, above.

56. Banerji, *Hour of the Goddess*.

57. Sil, "Ramakrishna-Vivekananda Research," 360.

58. See Kurtz, "In Our Image"; and Pintchman, "Is the Hindu Goddess a Good Resource?" 181–202.

59. Stepaniants, "Image of Woman in Religious Consciousness," 239–45.

60. Ganeshananda, "How the Holy Mother Influences Her Western Devotees," 495–96.

61. Chetanananda, *Matridarshan*, 65.

62. See Banerjee, "Marginalization of Women's Culture in Nineteenth-Century Bengal," 131.

63. Sastri, *Ramtanu Lahiri O Tatkalin Bangasamaj,* 52.

64. Cited in ibid., 53.

65. Roy, "Life and Teachings of Holy Mother Sarada Devi," 272.

66. See Mies, "Indian Women and Leadership," 56. Also, as Geraldine Forbes has demonstrated, even the Bengali nationalist revolutionaries had little problem in accepting females as their cohorts and on a par with the males. Forbes, "Goddesses or Rebels?" 1, 13 n. 2.

67. Her Devotee-Children, *Gospel of the Holy Mother*, 371.

68. Ishanananda, *Matrisanniddhye*, 162.

69. Mandavia, "Sarada Devi," 502ff.

70. Nivedita, *The Master as I Saw Him*, 150–51.

71. Her Devotee-Children, *Gospel of the Holy Mother*, 382 n. 1: reminiscences of Swami Ishanananda.

72. Gambhirananda, *Holy Mother Sri Sarada Devi*, 192–93.

73. Nikhilananda, *Holy Mother*, 6–15.

74. Ibid., 5–6.

75. Cited in Feldhaus, "Bahina Bai," 599.
76. Cited in Hallstrom, *Mother of Bliss*, 219.
77. Karlekar, *Voices from Within*, 136.
78. The Calcutta historian Dhurba Gupta has recently argued that the Renaissance model of an ideal woman—educated and cultivated for ideal wifehood—had its roots in the native culture of Hindu Bengal and had very little to do with Victorian morality and misogyny even though such a model was constructed in India in the reign of the British empress. See Gupta's analysis of the character of Bindubasini in Upendranath Das's play *Sharat-Sarojini* (1875) in "Jatiyatavad, Dharmiya Samkhyalaghutwa O Nari Prasanga." Gupta cites a contemporary review of this play that hails Bindubasini's character as an authentic representation of a true Indian (57).
79. Gambhirananda, *Holy Mother Sri Sarada Devi*, 6-7.
80. Ganesh, "Mother Who Is Not a Mother."
81. Pelikan, *Mary through the Centuries*, chap. 16.

GLOSSARY

Sources: Bhattacharyya, *Glossary of Religious Terms;* Kinsley, *Tantric Visions of Divine Feminine;* Sil, "Saradamani's Holy Motherhood"; idem, *Ramakrishna Revisited.*

APPENDIX A: HOLY MOTHER'S *LOGIA*

1. Ishanananda, *Matrisannidhye,* 107.
2. Ibid., 151.
3. Ibid.
4. Ibid., 162.
5. Ibid., 183.
6. Ibid., 113
7. Ibid., 123.
8. Ibid., 110.
9. Ibid., 35.
10. Ibid., 153.
11. Chetanananda, *Matridarshan,* 102.
12. Nikhilananda, *Sri Sarada Devi the Holy Mother (Conversations),* 248 (February 1914).
13. Ibid., 249 (22 July 1918).
14. Ibid., 253 (30 July 1918)
15. Ibid., 266 (3 September 1918).
16. Arupananda, *Srisrimayer Katha,* 295 (recorded by Dr. Umeshchandra Datta).
17. Ibid., 8 (July 1911, recorded by Sarayubala Devi).
18. Ibid., 17 (September 1912, recorded by Sarayubala Sen).
19. Ibid., 346 (recorded by Dr. Surendranath Roy).
20. Ibid., 78 (April 1919).
21. Ghosh, "Srisrisarada—'Kathamrita'," 540.
22. Ibid.
23. Ibid., 543.
24. Ibid., 544–45.
25. Ibid., 545.

26. Ibid.

27. Her Devotee-Children, *Gospel of the Holy Mother Sri Sarada Devi,* 151 (11 December 1912).

28. Ibid., 195 (conversation with Kshirodbala Roy).

29. Ibid., 301 (May 1915, recorded by an anonymous devotee).

30. Ibid., 305 (recorded by an anonymous devotee).

31. Ibid., 309 (recorded by Swami Vishweshwarananda).

32. Ibid., 318 (recorded by Swami Parameshwarananda).

33. Ibid., 322 (recorded by Nalinibehari Sarkar).

34. Ibid., 392 (c. 1909, recorded by Swami Ishanananda).

35. Ibid., 408 (c. 1909, recorded by Swami Ishanananda).

36. Ibid., 304 (May 1915, recorded by an anonymous devotee).

37. Purnatmananda, *Srisrimayer Padaprante,* 2:226 n. 2 (report of Swami Abhyananda).

38, Ibid., 2:398.

39. Dasgupta, *Saradadevi: Atmakatha,* 122.

Bibliography

WORKS IN BENGALI

Abjajananda, Swami. *Prakritim Paramam* [To the transcendent feminine]. 2 vols. Vol. 1 in 2 pts. Kalikata: Krishnanath Basu, 1397 B.E.

Akhandananda, Swami. *Smriti-katha* [Reminiscences]. 4th ed. Kalikata: Udbodhana Karyalaya, 1983.

Akshaychaitanya Brahmachari. *Srisrisaradadevi* [The Twice-blessed Sarada Devi]. 11th ed. Calcutta: Calcutta Book House Pvt., 1396 B.E.

————. *Thakur Sriramakrishna.* 3d ed. Calcutta: Calcutta Book House, 1393 B.E.

————, comp. *Swami Saradanander Patramala* [Letters of Swami Saradananda]. 2d ed. Kalikata: Brahmachari Akshaychaitnya, 1360 B.E.

Apurbananda, Swami. "Sriramakrishner 'Shakti'" [Sri Ramakrishna's power]. In *Shatarupe Sarada,* edited by Swami Lokeshwarananda, 1–13. Golpark: Ramakrishna Mission Institute of Culture, 1989.

Archanapuri, Sri. *Janani Saradeshwari.* [Sarada the Divine Mother]. 4th ed. Kalikata: Sri Satyananda Debayatan, 1992.

Arupananda, Swami. *Sriramakrishna O Srima* [Sri Ramakrishna and Sri Ma]. Bankura: Sri Ramakrishna Math, 1360 B.E.

————, comp. *Srisrimayer Katha* [Story of the Twice-blessed Mother]. 7th ed. Kalikata: Udbodhana Karyalaya, 1398 B.E.

Bandyopadhyay, Subhas. "Banglar Lokasamaskritir Dhara O Srima Sarada" [Patterns of Bengali folk culture and the Holy Mother Sarada]. In *Shatarupe Sarada,* edited by Swami Lokeshwarananda, 547–59. Golpark: Ramakrishna Mission Institute of Culture, 1989.

Barman, Gurudas. *Srisriramakrishnacharit* [Story of the Twice-blessed Ramakrishna]. 2 vols. Kalikata: Kalinath Singha, 1316 B.E.

Basu, Amritalal. *Bhagaban Sriramakrishnadever Balyalila* [The divine play of Lord Ramakrishna's childhood]. Calcutta: Basumati Rotary Press, 1330 B.E.

Basu, Rajsekhar, trans. *Krishnadwaipayaya Byaskrita Mahabharata* [Mahabharata by Krishnadwalpayan Byas]. Kalikata: n.p., 1958.

Basu, Shankariprasad. "Niveditar Dhrubamandir" [Nivedita's true temple]. In *Shatarupe Sarada,* edited by Swami Lokeshwarananda, 139–78. Golpark: Ramakrishna Mission Institute of Culture, 1989.

Basuray, Jyotirmay. "Srima: Sriramakrishner Dashjan Shisyer Dristite" [The Holy Mother as Sri Ramkrishna's ten disciples saw her]. In *Shatarupe Sarada,* edited by Swami Lokeshwarananda, 78–111. Golpark: Ramakrishna Mission Institute of Culture, 1989.

Bharadwaj, Nachiketa. "Saradadevi ebam Adhunikata" [Sarada Devi and modernity]. In *Shatarupe Sarada,* edited by Swami Lokeshwarananda, 525–37. Golpark: Ramakrishna Mission Institute of Culture, 1989.

Bharatiprana, Pravrjika. "Srisrimayer Charanaprante" [At the feet of the Twice-blessed Blessed Mother] In vol. 3 in *Srisrimayer Padaprante,* edited by Swami Purnatmananda, 510–21. Kalikata: Udbodhana Karyalaya, 1997.

Bhattacharya, Abhaychandra. *SriMar Jibandarshan* [SriM's outlook on life]. Kalikata: Grantha Bharati, 1397 B.E.

Bhattacharya, Bishnupada. "Bharatiya Chintadharay Shaktitatwa O Srisrima" [Shaktism in Indian thought and the Twice-blessed Mother]. In *Shatarupe Sarada,* edited by Swami Lokeshwarananda, 577–86. Golpark: Ramakrishna Mission Institute of Culture, 1989.

Bhumananda, Swami. *Srisrimayer Jiban-katha* [Story of the life of the Twice-blessed Mother]. Kalikata: Sriramakrishna-Sarada Math, 1986.

Budhananda, Swami. *Sriramakrishna-Bibhasita Ma Sarada* [Mother Sarada in the light of Sriramakrishna]. Kalikata: Udbodhana Karyalaya, 1996.

Chaitanyananda, Swami. "Sriramakrishna O Srisrima Saradadevi" [The Blessed Ramakrishna and the Twice-blessed Mother Saradadevi]. In *Bishwachetanay Sriramakrishna* [The Blessed Ramakrishna in global thought], edited by Swami Prameyananda et al., 325–54. 3d ed. Kalikata: Udbodhana Karyalaya, 1991.

Chakravarti, Niradbaran. "Radharupini" [Incarnation of Radha]. In *Shatarupe Sarada,* edited by Swami Lokeshwarananda, 687–95. Golpark: Ramakrishna Mission Institute of Culture, 1989.

Chetanananda, Swami, ed. *Matridarshan* [A View of the Mother]. 2d ed. Kalikata: Udbodhana Karyalaya, 1397 B.E.

Das, Shantiram. "Pisimar Katha" [An account of my aunt]. *Udbodhana* 98, no. 12 (Paus 1403 B.E.): 675–78.

Dasgupta, Abhaya, comp. *Saradadevi: Atmakatha* [Autobiographical talks of Saradadevi]. Golpark, Calcutta: Ramakrishna Mission Institute of Culture, 1979.

Dasgupta, Pranab K. *Prakriti-ma: Srisrisaradadevi* [Mother Nature: The Twice-blessed Saradadevi]. Kalikata: Jyoti Prakashan, 1382 B.E.

Dasgupta, Sudhirkumar. "Bharatiya Samaje Nari-Dharma" [Duties of women in Indian society]. *Udbodhana: Srisrima Shatabarsa Jayanti Sankhya* [The Twice-blessed Mother's birth centenary number], 1954, 46–50.

Datta, Chandramohan. "Punyasmriti." In vol. 1 of *Srisrimayer Padaprante,* edited by Swami Purnatmananda, 109–34. Kalikata: Udbodhana Karyalaya, 1994.

Datta, Mahendranath. *Srisriramakrishner Anudhyan* [Reflections on the Twice-blessed Ramakrishna]. Edited by Dhirendranath Basu. 6th ed. Calcutta: Mahendra Publishing Committtee, 1396 B.E.

Datta, Ramchandra. *Srisriramakrishna Paramahamsadever Jibanbrittanta* [Life of the Twice-blessed Ramakrishna Paramahamsa]. 8th ed. 1950. Reprint with minor rev., Kalikata: Udboshana Karyalaya, 1995.

Datta, Sureshchandra. *Srisriramakrishnadever Upadesh* [Sermons of the Twice-blessed Divine Ramakrishna]. 34th ed. Calcutta: Mitra Brothers, 1398 B.E.

De, Belarani. "Swayamvadini" [Her sayings]. In *Shatarupe Sarada,* edited by Swami Lokeshwarananda, 696–708. Golpark: Ramakrishna Mission Institute of Culture, 1989.

Debendranath, Swami. *Shantirupini Sarada* [Sarada: An image of peace]. Kalikata: Udbodhana Karyalaya, 1997.

Devi, Sridurgapuri. *Sarada-Ramakrishna.* Kalikata: Srisrisaradeshwari Ashrama, n.d.

Gangopadhyay, Sunil. *Sei Samay* [Those days]. 1st single vol. ed. Calcutta: Ananda Publishers, 1398 B.E.

Gaurishwarananda, Swami. "Ma Ke Yeman Dekhechhi." In *Shatarupe Sarada,* edited by Swami Lokeshwarananda, 251–60. Golpark: Ramakrishna Mission Institute of Culture, 1989.

Ghosal, Bipin B., comp. *Mukti ebam Tahar Sadhan* [Salvation and its attainment]. Kalikata: Udbodhana Karyalaya, 1393 B.E.

Ghosh, Manju. "Sahadharmini" [Helpmate]. In *Shatarupe Sarada,* edited by Swami Lokeshwarananda, 325–37. Golpark: Ramakrishna Mission Institute of Culture, 1989.

Ghosh, Pranabranjan. "Srisrisarada-'Kathamrita'" [Nectar of the sayings of the Twice-blessed Sarada]. In *Shatarupe Sarada,* edited by Swami Lokeshwarananda, 538–46. Golpark: Ramakrishna Mission Institute of Culture, 1989.

Gupta, Dhruba. "Jatiyatabad, Dharmiya Sankhyalaghutwa O Nari Prasanga" [On nationalism, religious minorities, and women]. *Sharadiya Anustup,* autumn 1996, 34–59.

Gupta, Mahendranath (SriM). *Srisriramakrishnakathamrita* [The nectar of the talks of the Twice-blessed Ramakrishna]. 5 *bhagas* [parts]. 1308–39 B.E. Reprint, Kalikata: Kathamrita Bhavana, 1394 B.E.

Hiranmayananda, Swami. "Swe Mahimni" [Unto her glory]. In *Shatarupe Sarada,* edited by Swami Lokeshwarananda, 637–42. Golpark: Ramakrishna Mission Institute of Culture, 1989.

Ishanananda, Swami. *Matrisannidhye* [In Mother's company]. 5th ed. Kalikata: Udbodhana Karyalaya, 1396 B.E.

Jagadishwarananda, Swami, comp. and ed. *Sriramakrishnaparsadprasanga* [On the associates of Sri Ramakrishna]. 1357 B.E. Reprint, Belur: Sriramakrishna Dharmachakra, 1398 B.E.

Kabiraj, Krishnadas. *Chaitanyacharitamrita* [The nectar of the life of Chaitanya]. Edited by Radhagobinda Nath. 6 vols. Kalikata: Bhaktiprachar Bhandar, 1949.

Lokeshwarananda, Swami. "Sanghajanani" [Mother of the order]. In *Shatarupe Sarada,* edited by Swami Lokeshwarananda, 366–87. Golpark: Ramakrishna Mission Institute of Culture, 1989.

Lokeshwarananda, Swami, ed. *Shatarupe Sarada* [The many faces of Sarada]. Golpark: Ramakrishna Mission Institute of Culture, 1989.

Matilal, Sanghaguru. *Sriramakrishner Dampatyajiban* [Married life of the Blessed Ramakrishna]. 2d ed. Calcutta: Pravartak Publishers, 1375 B.E.

Mitra, Ashutosh. "Srima" [Holy Mother]. In *Srisrimayer Padaprante,* edited by Swami Purnatmananda, 2:271–475. Kalikata: Udbodhana Karyalaya, 1995.

Mitra, Satyacharan. *Srisriramakrishna Paramahamsa (Jibani O Upadesh)* [The Twice-blessed Ramakrishna (life and teachings)]. Calcutta: Great India Press, 1308 B.E.

Mukherjee, Amitabha. "Nabajagaran, Samaj-Bibartan O Srima Saradadevi" [New awakening, social change, and the Holy Mother Sarada Devi]. In *Shatarupe Sarada,* edited by Swami Lokeshwarananda, 425–34. Golpark: Ramakrishna Mission Institute of Culture, 1989.

Mukhopadhyay, Govindagopal. "Shaktirupini" [Incarnation of Shakti]. In *Shatarupe Sarada*, edited by Swami Lokeshwarananda, 643–51. Golpark: Ramakrishna Mission Institute of Culture, 1989.

Mukhopadhyay, Jivan. "Bharater Swadhinata-Sangram: Srimayer Dristibhangi" [Holy Mother's outlook on the Indian struggle for independence]. In *Shatarupe Sarada*, edited by Swami Lokeshwarananda, 448–72. Golpark: Ramakrishna Mission Institute of Culture, 1989.

Muktiprana, Pravrajika. *Srima Sarada* [Holy Mother Sarada]. Dakshineswar: Srisarada Math, 1397 B.E.

Mumukshananda, Swami. "Srisrima: Prachin Adarsher Shes Pratinidhi ebam Nabin Adarsher Agradut" [The Twice-blessed Mother: Last representative of the old ideals and the herald of the new]. In *Shatarupe Sarada*, edited by Swami Lokeshwarananda, 587–608. Golpark: Ramakrishna Mission Institute of Culture, 1989.

Nag, Keshabehandra. "Kemane Bhuli Karuna Tanr" [How could I forget the Companion?]. In vol. 1 of *Srisrimayer Padaprante*, edited by Swami Purnatmananda, 93–95. Kalikata: Udbodhana Karyalaya, 1994.

Nirlepananda, Swami. *Ramakrishna Saradamrita* [The nectar of Ramakrishna and Sarada]. Kalikata: Karuna Prakashani, 1375 B.E.

Nirvanananda, Swami. "Matrisannidhye." In vol. 1 of *Srisrimayer Padaprante*, edited by Swami Purnatmananda, 23–27. Kalikata: Udbodhana Karyalaya, 1994.

Prabhananda, Swami. *Srisrisaradamahima* [Glory of the Twice-blessed Sarada]. Kalikata: Udbodhana Karyalaya, 1403 B.E.

Purnatmananda, Swami. *Chirantani Sarada* [Eternal Sarada]. Kalikata: Udbodhana Karyalaya, 1997.

———. "Sitarupini" [Incarnation of Sita]. In *Shatarupe Sarada*, edited by Swami Lokeshwarananda, 652–86. Golpark: Ramakrishna Mission Institute of Culture, 1989.

———, ed. *Srisrimayer Padaprante* [At the feet of the Twice-blessed Mother], 3 vols. Kalikata: Udbodhana Karyalaya, 1994–97.

Ray, Sarayu. "Kalkatay 'Mayer Badite' Ma ke Pratham Dekhi" [First meeting with Mother at her Calcutta residence]. In *Srisrimayer Padaprante*, edited by Swami Purnatmananda, 1:84–88. Kalikata: Udbodhana Karyalaya, 1994.

Sanyal, Vaikunthanath. *Srisriramakrishna Lilamrita* [The nectar of the divine play of the Twice-blessed Ramakrishna]. 1343 B.E. Reprint, Kalikata: Nabapatra Prakashan, 1390 B.E.

Saradananda, Swami. *Bharate Shaktipuja* [Shakti worship in India]. 9th ed. Kalikata: Udbodhana Karyalaya, 1365 B.E.

———. *Srisriramakrishnalilaprasanga* [The divine play of the Twice-blessed Ramakrishna]. 5 pts. in 2 vols. Kalikata: Udbodhana Karyalaya, 1398 B.E.

Saradeshananda, Swami. "Matrisamipe." In vol. 1 of *Srisrimayer Padaprante*, edited by Swami Purnatmananda, 3–22. Kalikata: Udbodhana Karyalaya, 1994.

———. *Srisrimayer Smritikatha* [Reminiscences of the Twice-blessed Mother]. 2d ed. Kalikata: Udbodhana Karyalaya, 1390 B.E.

Sarkar, Ramendranarayan. "Srima: Manisibrinder Dristite" [Holy Mother in the eyes of savants]. In *Shatarupe Sarada*, edited by Swami Lokeshwarananda, 217–37. Golpark: Ramakrishna Mission Institute of Culture, 1989.

Sastri, Sivanath. *Ramtanu Lahiri O Tatkalin Bangasamaj* [Ramtanu Lahiri and contemporary society in Bengal]. 3d ed. Calcutta: New Age Publishers, 1390 B.E.

Satswarupananda, Swami. "Karunamayi." In vol. 1 of *Srisrimayer Padaprante*, edited by Swami Purnatmananda, 62–67. Kalikata: Udbodhana Karyalaya, 1994.

Sen, Akshaykumar. *Sriramakrishnapunthi: Sriramakrishner Charitamrita*. 8th ed. Kalikata: Udbodhana Karyalaya, 1378 B.E.

Sengupta, Achintyakumar. *Paramaprakriti Srisri Saradamani*. 14th ed. Calcutta: Signet Press, 1394 B.E.

Someshwarananda, Swami. "Saradadevir Yuktinistha O Samajchetana" [Saradadevi's rationality and social consciousness]. In *Shatarupe Sarada*, edited by Swami Lokeshwarananda, 473–85. Golpark: Ramakrishna Mission Institute of Culture, 1989.

Sriarchanapuri. *Janani Saradeshwari* [Sarada the Divine Mother]. Jadavpur: Srisatyananda Devayatan, 1992.

Tejasananda, Swami. *Srisrima O Saptasadhika* [The Twice-blessed Mother and the seven ascetic women]. 2d ed. 1970. Reprint, Belur Math: Ramakrishna Mission Saradapith, 1993.

Vedantaprana, *Pravrajika*. "Lokajanani" [People's mother]. In *Shatarupe Sarada*, edited by Swami Lokeshwarananda, 308–24. Golpark: Ramakrishna Mission Institute of Culture, 1989.

Vivekananda, Swami. *Patrabali* [Letters]. 5th ed. Kalikata: Udbodhana Karyalaya, 1394 B.E.

WORKS IN ENGLISH AND FRENCH

Apte, V. M. "Social and Economic Conditions in the Age of the Rik Samhitas." In *The Vedic Age*, edited by Ramesh C. Majumdar and A.D. Pusalkar, 384–99. London: George Allen & Unwin, 1951.

Auerbach, Nina. *Women and the Dream: The Life of a Victorian Myth*. Cambridge: Harvard University Press, 1982.

Bagchi, Jasodhara. "Representing Nationalism: Ideology of Motherhood in Colonial Bengal." *Economic and Political Weekly* 25, nos. 42–43 (20–27 October 1990): WS 65–71.

Banerjee, Sumanta. "Marginalization of Women's Popular Culture in Nineteenth-Century Bengal." In *Recasting Women: Essays in Colonial History*, edited by Kumkum Sangari and and Sudesh Vaid, 127–79. New Delhi: Kali for Women, 1989.

Banerji, Chitrita. *The Hour of the Goddess: Memories of Women, Food, and Ritual in Bengal*. Calcutta: Seagull Books, 2001.

Bannerji, Himani. "Pygmalion Nation: Towards a Critique of Subaltern Studies and the 'Resolution of the Women's Question.'" In *Of Property and Propriety: The Role of Gender and Class in Imperialism and Nationalism*, edited by Himani Bannerji, Shahrzad Mojab, and Judith Whitehead, 34–84. Toronto: University of Toronto Press, 2001.

Bannerji, Himani, Shahrzad Mojab, and Judith Whitehead, eds. *Of Property and Propriety: The Role of Gender and Class in Imperialism and Nationalism*. Toronto: University of Toronto Press, 2001.

Bhagavad Gita [The song of God]. Translated by Swami Prabhavananda and Christopher Isherwood. 1944. Reprint, Hollywood, Calif.: Vedanta Press, 1987. Text citations are to the reprint edition.

Bharati, Agehandra. "The Hindu Renaissance and Its Apologetic Patterns." *Journal of Asian Studies* 29, no. 2 (February 1970): 267–87.

Bhattacharji, Sukumari. "Motherhood in Ancient India." *Economic and Political Weekly* 25, no. 42–43 (20–27 October 1990): WS 50–57.

Bhattacharyya, Narendra N. *A Glossary of Indian Religious Terms and Concepts.* New Delhi: Manohar Publications, 1990.

———. *History of the Tantric Religion.* 1982. Reprint, New Delhi: Manohar Publications, 1987.

Bilimoria, Purusottama, and Peter Fenner, eds. *Religions and Comparative Thought: Essays in Honour of the Late Dr. Ian Kesarkodi-Watson.* Delhi: Sri Satguru Publications, 1988.

Bose, Mandakranta, ed. *Faces of the Feminine in Ancient, Medieval, and Modern India.* New York: Oxford University Press, 2000.

Brain, James L. "Male Menstruation in History and Anthropology." *The Journal of Psychohistory* 15, no. 3 (1988): 311–24.

Brown, Charles B. *Wieland, or the Transformation.* Garden City, N.Y.: Doubleday & Co., 1962.

Bynum, Caroline W. *Holy Feast and Holy Fast: The Religious Significance of Food to Medieval Women.* Berkeley: University of California Press, 1987.

Canetti, Elias. *Crowds and Power.* Translated by Carol Stewart. New York: Viking Press, 1962. Cited in *Holy Feast and Holy Fast: The Religious Significance of Food to Medieval Women,* by Caroline W. Bynum. Berkeley: University of California Press, 1987.

Carstairs, George M. "Hinjra and Jiryan: Two Derivatives of Hindu Attitudes to Sexuality." *British Journal of Medical Psychology* 29, no. 2 (June 1956): 128–38.

Chatterjee, Partha. "The Nationalist Resolution of the Women's Question." In *Recasting Women: Essays in Colonial History,* edited by Kumkum Sangari and Sudesh Vaid, 233–53. New Deli: Kali for Women, 1989.

———. "A Religion of Urban Domesticity: Sri Ramakrishna and the Calcutta Middle Class." In *Subaltern Studies VII: Writings on South Asian History and Society,* edited by Partha Chatterjee and Gyanendra Pandey, 40–68. Delhi: Oxford University Press, 1992.

Chatterjee, Partha, and Gyanendra Pandey, eds. *Subaltern Studies VII: Writings on South Asian History and Society.* Delhi: Oxford University Press, 1992.

Chetanananda, Swami. *They Lived with God: Life Stories of Some Devotees of Sri Ramakrishna.* St. Louis, Mo.: Vedanta Society of St. Louis, 1989.

Cooey, Paula, William Eakin, and Jay McDaniel, eds. *After Patriarchy: Feminist Transformation of the World Religions.* Maryknoll, N.Y.: Orbis Books, 1991.

Copley, Antony, ed. *Gurus and Their Followers: New Religious Reform Movements in Colonial India.* New Delhi: Oxford University Press, 2000.

The Cultural Heritage of India: Sri Ramakrishna Centenary Memorial. 3 vols. Belur Math: Sri Ramakrishna Centenary Committee, c. 1936.

Denton, Lynn T. "Varieties of Hindu Female Asceticism." In *Roles and Rituals for Hindu Women,* edited by Julia Leslie, 211–31. Rutherford, N.J.: Fairleigh Dickinson University Press, 1991.

Dewart, Joanne. "Some Theoretical Aspects in the Writings of Laing." *Sciences Religieuses/ Studies in Religion* 3, no. 1 (1973): 63–70.

Dhar, Sailendra N. *A Comprehensive Biography of Swami Vivekananda.* 2d ed. 3 vols. in 2 pts. Madras: Vivekananda Prakashan Kendra, 1990.

Dimock, Edward. "Religious Biography in India: 'The Nectar of the Acts of Caitanya.'" In *The Biographical Process: Studies in the History and Psychology of Religion,* edited by

Frank Reynolds and Donald Capps, 109–17. Paris: Mouton, 1976.

Dumézil, Georges. *Mythe et Épopée.* 2 vols. Paris: Gallimard, 1971.

Erikson, Erik H. *Identity: Youth and Crisis.* New York:: W. W. Norton & Co., 1968.

Feldhaus, Anne. "Bahina Bai: Wife and Saint." *Journal of the American Academy of Religion* 50, no. 4 (December 1982): 593–604.

Forbes, Geraldine. "Goddesses or Rebels? The Women Revolutionaries of Bengal." *Oracle* 2, no. 4 (April 1980): 1–15.

———. "The Ideals of Indian Womanhood: Six Bengali Women during the Independence Movement." In *Bengal in the Nineteenth and Twentieth Centuries,* edited by John R. McLane, 59–74. East Lansing: Michigan State University Press, 1975.

Gambhirananda, Swami. *Holy Mother Sri Sarada Devi.* Mylapore: Sri Ramakrishna Math, 1977.

Ganesh, Kamala. "Mother Who Is Not a Mother: In Search of the Great Indian Goddess." *Economic and Political Weekly* 25, nos. 42–43 (20–27 October 1990): WS 58–64.

Ganeshananda, Swami. "How the Holy Mother Influences Her Western Devotees." *Prabuddha Bharata* 89 (December 1984): 491–97.

Gatwood, Lynn E. *Devi and the Spouse Goddess: Women, Sexuality, and Marriages in India.* Riverdale, N.Y.: Riverdale Co., 1985.

Ghanananda, Swami. "Sri Sarada Devi the Holy Mother." In *Women Saints of East and West: Sri Sarada Devi (The Holy Mother) Birth Centenary Memorial,* edited by Swami Ghanananda and John Stewart-Wallace, 94–121. London: Ramakrishna Vedanta Centre, 1953.

Green, Richard, and John Money, eds. *Transsexualism and Sex Reassignment.* Baltimore: Johns Hopkins University Press, 1969.

Gupta, Lina. "Kali the Savior." In *After Patriarchy: Feminist Transformation of the World Religions,* edited by Paula Cooey, William Eakin, and Jay McDaniel, 15–38. Maryknoll, N.Y.: Orbis Books, 1991.

Gupta, Samjukta. "The Goddess, Women, and Their Rituals in Hinduism." In *Faces of Feminine in Ancient, Medieval, and Modern India,* edited by Mandakranta Bose, 87–106. New York: Oxford University Press, 2000.

———. "Women in the Shaiva/Shakta Ethos." In *Roles and Rituals for Hindu Women,* edited by Julia Leslie, 193–209. Rutherford, N.J.: Fairleigh Dickinson University Press, 1991.

Haberman, David L. *Acting as a Way of Salvation: A Study of Raganuga Bhakti.* New York: Oxford University Press, 1988.

———. "Imitating the Masters: Problems in Incongruity." *Journal of the American Academy of Religion* 53, no. 1 (1985): 41–49.

Hallstrom, Lisa L. *Mother of Bliss: Anandamayi Ma, 1896–1982.* New York: Oxford University Press, 1999.

Her Devotee-Children. *The Gospel of the Holy Mother Sri Sarada Devi.* Madras: Sri Ramakrishna Math, 1984.

Hiltebeitel, Alf, and Kathleen M. Erndl, eds. *Is the Goddess a Feminist? The Politics of South Asian Goddesses.* New York: New York University Press, 2000.

Hiranmayananda, Swami. "The Holy Mother Ideal." *Prabuddha Bharata* 90 (March 1985): 105–10.

"Holy Mother–Ideal of Womanhood." *Prabuddha Bharata* 44 (December 1989): 482–91. Editorial.

Hughes, Maeve. *Epic Women East and West: A Study with Special Reference to the Mahabharata and Celtic Heroic Literature*. Calcutta: Asiatic Society, 1994.

Jacobson, Knut A. "The Female Pole of the Godhead in Tantrism and the *Prakriti* of Samkhya." *Numen: International Review of the History of Religions* 43, no. 1 (January 1966): 56–81.

Kakar, Sudhir. *Shamans, Mystics, and Doctors: A Psychological Inquiry into India and Its Healing Traditions*. New York: Alfred A. Knopf, 1982.

Karlekar, Malavika. *Voices from Within: Personal Narratives of Bengali Women*. New Delhi: Oxford University Press, 1990.

Khandelwal, Meena. "Ungendered *Atma*, Masculine Virility, and Feminine Compassion: Ambiguities in Renunciant Discourses on Gender." *Contributions to Indian Sociology*, n.s., 21, no. 1 (1997): 79–107.

Kinsley, David. *Tantric Visions of the Divine Feminine: The Ten Mahavidyas*. Berkeley: University of California Press, 1997.

Kopf, David. "The Brahmo Idea of Social Reform and the Problem of Female Emancipation in Bengal." In *Bengal in the Nineteenth and Twentieth Centuries,* edited by John R. McLane, 35–58. East Lansing: Michigan State University Press, 1975.

Kripal, Jeffrey J. *Kali's Child: The Mystical and the Erotic in the Life and Teachings of Ramakrishna*. Chicago: University of Chicago Press, 1995.

———. "Perfecting the Mother's Silence: Dream, Devotion, and Family in the Deification of Sharada [*sic*] Devi." In *Seeking Mahadevi: Constructing the Identities of the Hindu Great Goddess,* edited by Tracy Pintchman, 171–97. Albany: State University of New York Press, 2001.

Kurtz, Stanley. "In Our Image: The Feminist Vision of the Hindu Goddess." In *Is the Goddess a Feminist? The Politics of South Asian Goddesses*, edited by Alf Hiltebeitel and Kathleen M. Erndl, 181–86. New York: New York University Press, 2000.

Laing, R. D. *The Divided Self*. New York: Pantheon Books, 1960.

Leslie, Julia. "Sri and Jyeshtha: Ambivalent Role Models for Women." In *Roles and Rituals for Hindu Women,* edited by Julia Leslie, 107–37. Rutherford, N.J.: Fairleigh Dickinson University Press, 1991.

———, ed. *Roles and Rituals for Hindu Women*. Rutherford, N.J.: Fairleigh Dickinson University Press, 1991.

Life of Sri Ramakrishna Compiled from Various Authentic Sources. 2d ed. Calcutta: Advaita Ashrama, 1928.

Majumdar, Ramesh C. *The Vedic Age*. Vol. 1 of *The History and Culture of the Indian People*. Bombay: Bharatiya Vidya Bhavan, 1965.

Mandavia, Chetna. "Sri Sarada Devi: An Ideal for Modern Women." *Prabuddha Bharata* 45 (December 1990): 500–506.

Masson, Jeffrey M. "The Psychology of the Ascetic." *Journal of Asian Studies* 35, no. 4 (August 1976): 611–25.

McDaniel, June. *Madness of the Saints: Ecstatic Religion in Bengal*. Chicago: University of Chicago Press, 1989.

McDermott, Rachel F. "Evidence for the Transformation of the Goddess Kali: Kamalakanta Bhattacharya and the Shakta Padavali." Ph.D. dissertation, Harvard University, 1993.

———. *Mother of My Heart, Daughter of My Dreams: Kali and Uma in the Devotional Poetry of Bengal*. New York: Oxford University Press, 2001.

McKibbin, Penelope. "The Personality of Prakriti—Keys to a Feminist Predicament." In *Religions and Comparative Thought: Essays in Honour of the Late Dr. Ian Kesarkodi-Watson,* edited by Purusottama Bilimoria and Peter Fenner, 265–84. Delhi: Sri Satguru Publications, 1988.

McLane, John R., ed. *Bengal in the Nineteenth and Twentieth Centuries.* East Lansing: Michigan State University Press, 1975.

McLean, Malcolm D. "Women as Aspects of the Mother Goddess in India: A Case Study of Ramakrishna." *Religion* 19 (1989): 13–26.

Meissner, W. W. *The Psychology of a Saint: Ignatius of Loyola.* New Haven: Yale University Press, 1992.

Mies, Maria. "Indian Women and Leadership." *Bulletin of Concerned Asian Scholars* 7, no. 1 (January–March 1975): 56–66.

Money, John. *Venuses Penuses: Sexology, Sexosophy, and Exigency Theory.* Buffalo, N.Y.: Prometheus Books, 1986.

Mookerjee, Nanda, ed. *Sri Ramakrishna in the Eyes of Brahmo and Christian Admirers.* Calcutta: Firma KLM Pvt., 1976.

———, ed. *Sri Sarada Devi, Consort of Sri Ramakrishna.* Calcutta: Firma KLM Pvt., 1978.

Mozoomdar, Protap. "Paramahamsa Srimat Ramakrishna." *Theistic Quarterly Review,* October–December 1879, 32–39.

Mukharji, Prasanta B. "Sarada Devi: A Centenary Tribute." *Prabuddha Bharata,* March 1954, 131–37.

Müller, Friedrich Max. *Ramakrishna: His Life and Sayings.* 1899. Reprint, New York: AMS Press, 1975. Text citations are to the reprint edition.

Nikhilananda, Swami. *Holy Mother: Being the Life of Sri Sarada Devi, Wife of Ramakrishna and Helpmate in His Mission.* 2d ed. New York: Ramakrishna-Vedanta Center, 1982.

———, trans. *Sri Sarada Devi the Holy Mother (Book II: Her Conversations).* Mylapore: Sri Ramakrishna Math, 1980.

Nirvedananda, Swami. "Sri Ramakrishna and Spiritual Renaissance." In *The Cultural Heritage of India: Sri Ramakrishna Centenary Memorial,* 2:441–617. 3 vols. Belur Math: Sri Ramakrishna Centenary Committee, c. 1936.

Nivedita, Sister. *Letters of Nivedita.* Edited by Sankari P. Basu. 2 vols. Calcutta: Navabharat Publishers, 1982.

———. *The Master as I Saw Him: Being Pages from the Life of the Swami Vivekananda by His Disciple Nivedita, of Ramakrishna-Vivekananda.* 1918. Reprint, New York: Longmans, Green & Co., 1919.

Ojha, Catherine. "Feminine Asceticism in Hinduism: Its Traditions and Present Condition." *Man in India,* nos. 61–63 (September 1981): 254–85.

Pandey, Asha Lata. "Hindu View on Women." *Dharma-marg: A Quarterly Journal of the Vedic Research and Cultural Foundation,* July 2002, 43–45.

Pauly, Ira B. "Adult Manifestation of Male Transsexualism." In *Transsexualism and Sex Reaasignment,* edited by Richard Green and John Money, 37–58. Baltimore: Johns Hopkins University Press, 1969.

Pelikan, Jaroslav. *Mary through the Centuries.* New Haven: Yale University Press, 1996.

Pintchman, Tracy. "Is the Hindu Goddess Tradition a Good Resource for Western Feminism?" In *Is the Goddess a Feminist? The Politics of South Asian Goddesses,* edited by Alf Hiltebeitel and Kathleen M. Erndl, 187–202. New York: New York University Press, 2000.

————, ed. *Seeking Mahadevi: Constructing the Identities of the Hindu Great Goddess.* Albany: State University of New York Press, 2001.

Prabhananda, Swami. *First Meetings with Sri Ramakrishna.* Mylapore: Sri Ramakrishna Math, 1987.

————. "Swami Vivekananda and His 'Only Mother'." *Prabuddha Bharata* 89 (January 1984): 10–20.

Ray, Rajat K., ed. *Mind, Body, and Society: Life and Mentality in Colonial Bengal.* Calcutta: Oxford University Press, 1995.

Reynolds, Frank, and Donald Capps, eds. *The Biographical Process: Studies in the History and Psychology of Religion.* Paris: Mouton, 1976.

Rinehart, Robin. *One Lifetime, Many Lives: The Experience of Modern Hindu Hagiography.* Atlanta, Ga.: Scholars Press, 1999.

Robinson, Betty Sue. "The Ramakrishna Sarada Math: A Study of a Women's Movement in Bengal." Ph.D. dissertation, Columbia University, 1978.

Rolland, Romain. *The Life of Ramakrishna.* Calcutta: Advaita Ashrama, 1928.

Roy, Shreela. "Life and Teachings of Holy Mother Sri Sarada Devi: The Relevance for the Modern Indian Women." *Bulletin of the Ramakrishna Mission Institute of Culture* 35, no. 12 (December 1984): 272–77.

Rudolph, Lloyd I., and Susan H. Rudolph. *The Modernity of Tradition: Political Development in India.* Chicago: University of Chicago Press, 1967.

Rüstau, Hiltrud. "The Ramakrishna Mission: Its Female Aspect." In *Gurus and Their Followers: New Religious Reform Movements in Colonial India,* edited by Antony Copley, 83–103. New Delhi: Oxford University Press, 2000.

Samanta, Suchitra. "*Mangalmayima, Sumangali, Mangal:* Bengali Perceptions of the Divine Feminine, Motherhood, and Auspiciousness." *Contributions to Indian Sociology* 26, no. 1 (1992): 51–75.

Sangari, Kumkum, and Sudesh Vaid, eds. *Recasting Women: Essays in Colonial History.* New Delhi: Kali for Women, 1989.

Sarkar, Sumit. "'Kaliyuga', 'Chakri,' and 'Bhakti': Ramakrishna and His Time." *Economic and Political Weekly* 27, no. 28 (18 July 1992): 1543–66.

Sarkar, Tanika. "Nationalist Iconography: Image of Woman in the Nineteenth-Century Bengali Literature." *Economic and Political Weekly* 22, no. 47 (21 November 1987): WS 2011–51.

Sil, Narasingha P. "Misogyny and Asceticism: Vivekananda's Concept of Woman." *Asian Culture Quarterly* 25, no. 2 (summer 1997): 37–53.

————. "Ramakrishna-Vivekananda Research: Hagiography versus Hermeneutics." *Religious Studies Review* 27, no. 4 (October 2001): 355–62.

————. *Ramakrishna Revisited: A New Biography.* Lanham, Md.: University Press of America, 1998.

————. "Saradamani the Holy Mother: The Making of a Madonna." *Asian Culture Quarterly* 21, no. 2 (summer 1993): 71–81.

————. "Saradamani's Holy Motherhood: A Reappraisal." *Asian Journal of Women's Studies* 4, no. 1 (1998): 33–76.

————. "Saradamani's Missed Motherhood vs. Holy Motherhood." *Journal of Religious Studies* 28, no. 1 (spring 1997): 64–84.

————. *Swami Vivekananda: A Reassessment.* Selinsgrove, Pa.: Susquehanna University Press, 1997.

———. "Vivekananda's Ramakrishna: An Untold Story of Mythmaking and Propaganda." *Numen: International Review of the History of Religions* 40, no. 1 (1993): 38–62.

Smith, Frederick M. "Indra's Curse, Varuna's Noose, and the Suppression of the Woman in the Vedic Srauta Ritual." In *Roles and Rituals for Hindu Women*, edited by Julia Leslie, 17–45. Rutherford, N.J.: Fairleigh Dickinson University Press, 1991.

Spratt, Philip. *Hindu Culture and Personality: A Psycho-Analytic Study.* Bombay: P.C. Manaktala & Sons Pvt., 1966.

Sri Sarada Devi the Holy Mother: Being the Life and Teachings of One Whose Mission It Was to Reveal the Motherhood of God. Mylapore: Sri Ramakrishna Math, 1949.

Stepaniants, M. T. "The Image of Woman in Religious Consciousness: Past, Present, and Future." *Philosophy Past and Present* 42, no. 2 (1992): 239–47.

Tagore, Rabindranath. *A Tagore Testament.* Translated by Indu Dutt. Bombay: Jaico Publishing House, 1969.

Tapasyananda, Swami. *Sri Ramakrishna: Life and Teachings (An Interpretive Study).* Mylapore: Sri Ramakrishna Math, 1983.

———. *Sri Sarada Devi the Holy Mother: Life and Teachings.* Mylapore: Sri Ramakrishna Math, 1982.

Tawney, Charles H. *A Modern Hindu Saint.* Calcutta: S. C. Mitra, 1897.

Vivekananda, Swami. *The Complete Works of Swami Vivekananda.* Mayavati Memorial ed. 8 vols. Reprint, Calcutta: Advaita Ashrama, 1989.

Wadley, Susan S. "Paradoxical Powers of Tamil Women." In *The Powers of Tamil Women,* edited by Susan S. Wadley, 153–67. South Asian Series no. 6. Syracuse, N.Y.: Syracuse University Press, 1980.

———. "Women and the Hindu Tradition." *Signs: Journal of Women in Culture and Society* 3, no. 1 (autumn 1977): 113–25.

———. "Women and the Hindu Tradition." In *Women in India: Two Perspectives,* edited by Doranne Jacobson and Susan S. Wadley, 111–35. Columbia, Mo.: South Asia Publications, 1992. (This is a fuller version of the *Signs* article mentioned above.)

———, ed. *The Powers of Tamil Women.* South Asian Series no. 6. Syracuse, N.Y.: Syracuse University Press, 1980.

Walsh, Judith. "The Virtuous Wife and the Well-Ordered Home: The Re-conceptualization of Bengali Women and their Worlds." In *Mind, Body, and Society: Life and Mentality in Colonial Bengal,* edited by Rajat K. Ray, 331–63. Calcutta: Oxford University Press, 1995.

Index

WITHDRAWN